The Columbia River's
"Ellis Island"
The Story of Knappton Cove

The Columbia River Quarantine Station – 1903

Original Edition © 2002 by Nancy Bell Anderson
Revised Edition © 2012 by Nancy Bell Anderson, Edited by Heather Bell Henry

The Columbia River's "Ellis Island"

The Story of Knappton Cove

Columbia River Quarantine Station at Knappton Cove 1899-1938

By Nancy Bell Anderson

Edited by Heather Bell Henry

Heritage Folk Press

www.heritagefolk.com

Dedicated to the thousands of folks who, through the centuries, have stood on these shores—drawing strength and inspiration from this great river.

"Far away on the open sea,
Lies a place for you and me,
Beyond my childhood history,
A place of mystery."

~Rev. Dr. Ken Henry

TABLE OF CONTENTS

Special thanks to *Patrick Hammersmith*, whose photography skills brought back to life old glass photo plates from the archives of the Columbia River Maritime Museum. Twelve of those vintage photos appear inside these covers. And, thanks to *Carlton Appelo*, historian extraordinaire—for inspiration.

FOREWARD

This historic site has such an interesting story—one that has not been fully recorded. Since it's been a significant part of my life for over fifty years, I felt compelled to *WRITE IT DOWN*. Which is what I've done.

The Astorian newspaper printed this article in June of 1950 announcing that the old Government Quarantine Station near Knappton was on the auction block. It was described as "Suitable for Resort" and went on to state that, ironically, its original guests were not always willing ones. Federal legislation in 1891 had mandated the medical inspection of all arriving immigrants in an effort to control the spread of communicable diseases. Although Ellis Island handled the largest number of immigrants, there were other ports of entry. The Columbia River was one of only four major ports of entry on the west coast.

Historic Knappton Quarantine Station For Sale

The old Columbia river quarantine station near Knappton is on the block for sale, the surplus disposal service of the federal government revealed Wednesday.

"Suitable for resort" is one of the descriptive phrases used ironically since the station was a brief-vacation site for countless immigrants and mariners during the first decades of this century, though its guests were not always willing ones.

The entire plant was declared surplus by the U. S. public health service in 1936, and was transferred to coast guard ownership May 30, 1942.

The station was established May 9, 1899, by Asst. Surgeon Hill Hastings. Sulphur was used in a two-day fumigation of ships until cyanide replaced the slower chemical, and the hull of the old navy cruiser Concord served many years to house arriving passengers and crew members suspected of carrying disease.

The station includes 4½ acres of land, a dock with the fumigation building and equipment at its offshore end, attendants' quarters, a barn, a cookhouse, and the hospital itself.

Bids will be received, the announcement said, until July 14 at general services administration headquarters in Seattle.

From *The Astorian*—June 1, 1950

Photos taken of the Station by the
Bell Family around 1950

Notice Portions of the Old Boardwalk

THE BELLS AT KNAPPTON COVE CAMP 1950-1987
SPORT FISHING

Knappton Cove – a lonely spot on the north shore of the lower Columbia River estuary – became an important part of my life in 1950, the summer I turned 12. Our family lived in Portland where Dad, Clarence V. Bell, was Foreman of the Automotive Department at Benson Polytechnic High School for Boys. Dad was an avid outdoorsman. Hunting and fishing were his passions. Every August our family spent 2 weeks camping and salmon fishing at McGowan's Landing in Washington near the mouth of the Columbia River. Our boat was a 14' BIRCHCRAFT with a 15 H.P. EVINRUDE outboard motor. Dad and my two older brothers, Tom and Bob, fished and Mom canned the salmon. All our friends and relatives got our home-canned salmon for Christmas.

My older brother Tom was always looking for surplus stuff to buy. He'd get these GSA (General Services Administration) lists and bid on some very strange things. In 1950 one of those lists advertised an old deserted Quarantine Station for sale – accessible only by an 8-mile dead-end gravel road from Naselle, Washington or by boat. It occupied 4 1/2 acres on the banks of the Columbia directly across the river from Astoria, Oregon and included 7 acres of tideland. He told Dad about it and upon investigation, they decided it would make a suitable site for a summer Sport Fishing Camp & Moorage. There were several buildings on shore: a 2-story house, an old Quarantine Hospital, a Mess Hall, a Workshop, a Generator House, and a redwood water tower and storage tank. The buildings were in fair shape, and there was a large dock building (250' x 60') and approach (740'x 10' gangway) to the wharf as well. Dad was a genuine jack-of-all-trades. He could fix just about anything. He could do wiring, plumbing and carpentry. He knew motors backwards and forwards. Nothing intimidated him. So he talked one of his teaching friends into going 50-50 with him on a bid for the old Station. At $5,000 theirs was the winning bid, and **Knappton Cove Camp** was born. Mom decided on the name because of the little cove's location just a short way downriver from the old town site of Knappton. The name *Knappton Cove* stuck and has been in common use since 1950.

And the work began…and the three-hour drives every weekend from our home in NE Portland – across the interstate bridge through Vancouver, Washington and on to Longview. Since we always left Friday as soon as school was out, we'd arrive in Longview just about dinnertime and Dad would treat us

Some BIG Ones! Bob Jones, Mom, Dad and Me

Tom Bell with Big Salmon

Tom Bell, Bernita Zimmerman, Bob Jones

COLUMBIA CHINOOK SALMON River 1941 Christmas

NANCY MOM

TOM DAD BOB CAUGHT AND CANNED by the 9's

Merry

Dad's 1941 Homemade
Salmon Can Label.
I got to do the coloring.

LUCKY LOUIE by Bill Minser

SALMON PLUGS
from the 50's
Lucky Louie's
"Pearl Pink" was

The HOT salmon plug!!!

Salmon Derby Brochure—1953

GRAND PRIZE

Largest Fish Caught in Derby **$1000.00**
Plus Trophy

Largest Fish Caught Each Day **$100.00**
Plus Trophy

Second Largest Fish
Caught Each Day **$50.00**

Largest Fish Caught
By Woman in Derby **$100.00**

* *

SPONSORED BY

CHINOOK PROGRESSIVE CLUB

* *

WEIGHING-IN STATIONS

Astoria Salmon Derby Hdqs., foot 16th st., Astoria, Ore.
Hendrickson Moorage .... Warrenton, Ore.
Chinook Post Office Store .... Chinook, Wn.

CHINOOK
SALMON DERBY

AUGUST 29 to SEPT. 7 incl.

1953

$2,600.00

Plus Trophies

*"The Best Salmon Fishing
in the World"*

CHINOOK, WASHINGTON

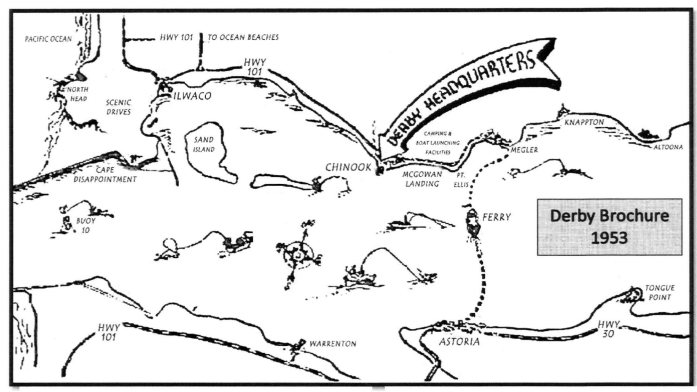

Derby Brochure 1953

RULES OF DERBY

FISHING PLACE: On Columbia River between Altoona, Washington, and the Columbia River Bar inside Buoy 10.

REGISTRATION FEES: All persons participating in the Derby must pay an entry fee of $2.00 good for the duration of the Derby.

REGISTRATION REQUIREMENTS: Fish must be caught in presence of a witness occupying same boat who must accompany angler to weighing-in station and who must also be registered in the Derby.

WEIGHING-IN PLACE AND TIME: All fish to be weighted must be brought to an official weighing-in station, between the hours of 12:00 noon and 7:00 p.m.

PACIFIC STANDARD TIME

North Shore Station—Post Office Store, Chinook, Wn.
Astoria Station—Astoria Salmon Derby Hdqs., foot of 16th St.
Warrenton Station—Hendrickson Moorage.

WEIGHING-IN RULES: All fish to be entered in Derby must be presented and weighed on the day caught. Any fish may be opened for inspection by an Official of the Derby after weighing.

USE OF HAND LINES: (MEAT LINES) IN ANY CRAFT—EITHER BY BOAT OPERATOR OR CONTESTANTS, DISQUALIFIES ALL OCCUPANTS FROM PARTICIPATION IN DERBY PRIZES

TACKLE REQUIREMENTS

All fish must be caught on Rod and Reel.

All fishermen must comply with the Oregon or Washington State Angling Laws.

Each contestant shall be permitted assistance in gaffing his or her fish, but no assistance may be given at any time in handling of rod or line.

Violation of any rules of this contest will eliminate the violator and all decisions made by the judges in regard to violations will be final.

In the event of a tie in daily or final weighing, the winner shall be determined by toss of a coin.

Participants in Derby must furnish own gear.

Boat Rates will be reasonable and standardized.

Decision of the Judges Shall Be Final

For Boat Reservations and Further Information, Write To Chinook Salmon Derby Committee

Chinook, Washington

4

to great hamburgers at the In 'n Out drive-in. Then we continued on past Cathlamet, Puget Island, and Skamokawa to Naselle where we finally reached the old Knappton Road, unpaved and 8 miles until it dead-ended just behind the Station. We'd work all weekend – or in my case, mostly play – until the return trip back to Portland late Sunday afternoon. What a relief when summer vacation arrived and those drives were less frequent. We pretty much spent all summer there gearing up for August when the sport fishermen (and women) arrived. Early on, Dad had a falling out with his partner (due, as I remember, to a 'new' wife) and he bought out George Brown's half. It rankled him that he had to pay George $5,000 to buy him out, financed by taking out a second mortgage on our Portland home.

Part of Dad's 'maintenance crew' were the few neighboring gillnet fishermen who lived in this remote area. Harold Hagerup, Ed Smalley and Charley Mattson had moored their gillnetters at the dock for years. Dad was grateful for their experienced help. In exchange for moorage, they assisted with the dock maintenance. Charley lived with his wife Cora right next to the Station. Ed, a bachelor, became our caretaker, taking up residence in the building that had served as the Mess Hall, converting it to a small home. Harold was a classic Norwegian bachelor, living at the family home just west of the Station with his mother – who everybody called Grandma Hagerup. Indeed, her grandchildren often came on weekends from Wauna to visit. I always looked forward to their arrival because it meant I had other kids to keep me company – the twins, Clara and Larry and their older brothers, Ben and Arnold Sorensen, and their cousins Shirley and Joe Higgins.

We had such fun playing on the beach and the dock, exploring the nearby woods and swimming in the river. The twins were real daredevils. They jumped around from log to log like gazelles, Larry usually in the lead with Clara – her blonde braids flying – close behind. Sometimes we would hide under the approach to the dock and smoke something the twins called 'smokewood' – porous bits of driftwood about the size of a cigar. We spent a good deal of time out on the dock fishing for suckers. They showed me how to make bread balls to use for bait. We'd have contests to see who could catch the most, lining them up on the dock as we brought them in. Then we'd throw the dead fish to the seagulls. On a rainy day, we'd play board games at the Hagerups and records on their old wind-up Victrola. They were a fun-loving group – always lots of joking, teasing and laughter. Grandma Hagerup herself was a real live wire. She baked bread every day and always had something home-baked to offer you. She also gave me steamy romance novels to read that I hid from my mother!

ENTRY SIGN TO KNAPPTON COVE CAMP

This sign hung above the entry to the camp from the old county road that ended behind the hospital building. The sign now hangs in the museum.

Boats Moored at Dock ~ 1950's
Note 2 Gillnet Boats

Boat Being Launched
Note Tents & Trailer in
Campground

BOAT LAUNCHING 2⁰⁰ Per Day

Winter at Knappton Cove
Note Drift on Beach and *No Highway*

CHINOOK SALMON DERBY
AUGUST 27 TO SEPTEMBER 5 INCLUSIVE
1955
$2350.
IN CASH PRIZES PLUS TROPHIES

Top Row: Bernita Zimmerman, Me, Mom, Ed Smalley
Center: Harold Hagerup & Dad
Bottom: Orville Zimmerman & Charley Mattson

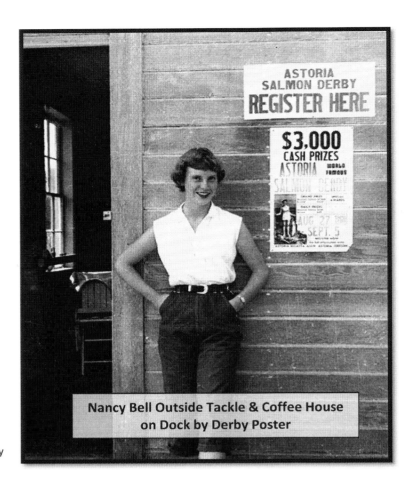

Nancy Bell Outside Tackle & Coffee House
on Dock by Derby Poster

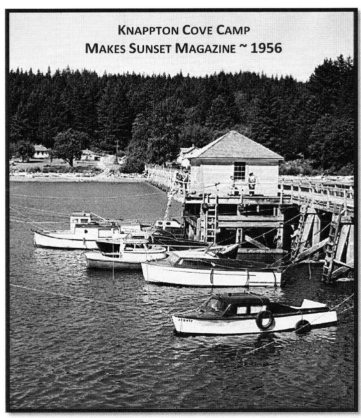

**KNAPPTON COVE CAMP
MAKES SUNSET MAGAZINE ~ 1956**

**Tom Bell, Unknown Lady & Clarence Bell
Outside Tackle House
By "Wallace Highliner" Sign**

"Uncle Harold" was a great guy. He frequently took us places in his boat – to the ferry landing on Sundays to buy the Sunday paper and treat us to ice cream cones, or to Astoria so we could take in a movie. Sometimes he took us all out to fish for tom-cod, a delicate white-meat fish that was delicious fried. That was really fun. We'd bait several hooks and bring up 3 or 4 little fish at the same time. Since the tom-cod only took the bait just before and around the turn of the tide, the action didn't last long. Once he took us out for a night drift when the salmon were running. It was a beautiful moonlit night – one I'll always remember. The silver fish flashed in the moonlight as the net lifted them over the side of the boat and the lights of Astoria twinkled in the distance. We went on longer day trips, too – upriver to Frankfort (a ghost town), Cathlamet, Westport, Wauna (where the Sorensens and Higgins lived), and Puget Island. And every Fourth of July, we had a big bonfire on the beach complete with fireworks. The twins also taught me how to throw a lit firecracker off the dock so it would explode just as it hit the water. Of course, Mom never knew about that! What great experiences for me – a city kid!

As the sport fishing season approached, the campground filled with tents and cars, and boats lined the dock. The price was $2 a day and $20 a season for a tent site and boat moorage. Dad set me up in business out on the pier in the little building that had been the pumphouse. We sold fishing tackle, Boyd's coffee, candy bars and chances on the 'derby.' The 'hot' salmon fishing plug at the time was a 'Lucky Louie Pearl Pink,' but the Ferry Landing held the local franchise on Lucky Louie, so we had to settle for Wallace Highliners. I developed a pretty good sales pitch for those plugs! Dad got me a little motorized "Doodlebug" so I could run errands for him. I just loved racing that little cycle back and forth on the pier.

Every fisherman dreamed of winning the annual Chinook Salmon Derby. In 1952 and '53 the biggest salmon of the day brought $100, and the Grand Prize for the season got you $1,000. The 1952 winner was Ken Carpenter from Portland with a 49 lbs.13 0z Chinook, and the '53 winner was Floy Nelson with a 50 lbs. 9 1/4 oz. whopper. In 1955 trophies were added.

Business was good, and Dad was having the time of his life. Profits from the business helped put me through Oregon State College. In 1956, Knappton Cove Camp even made Sunset Magazine. For the rest of his life, Knappton Cove was Dad's pride and joy. He and Mom started fixing up the old house on the property for their retirement.

Then came a blow. The Army Corps of Engineers began surveying for a road to link the Knappton Road (Hwy 401) to Megler where the ferry operated between Oregon and Washington (Hwy 101). Much to our dismay, it was decided to build the road along the waterfront – right through the front of our property – cutting off direct access to the dock and our river beach. It also effectively cut off our swimming hole. *'Acquisition by Condemnation'* is what it's called. What a bummer. The new highway was completed in 1960. The folks newly remodeled home had to be moved back 32 feet to allow for the highway. Moving the house and putting up a chain-link fence and gate across the entrance to our river beach was the only compensation they received. But my folks went ahead with their retirement plans, sold their Portland home, and moved permanently to Knappton in 1966. They took great pride in maintaining a beautiful parklike setting. My husband Rex and I were even married there – on Friday the 13th of July, 1962. And after the wedding, "Uncle Harold" took us across the river in his gillnetter to Astoria where Rex had parked his car. He always took the ferry channel so there we were – me in my white wedding suit and Rex with a bottle of champagne standing atop the fish nets in the bow of the boat – waving to the ferry passengers as Harold whizzed by (or so it seemed at the time) past the M.R. Chessman plying its way to Astoria. Rex was amazed at the ease with which Harold maneuvered that boat.

By 1970, storms had battered the dock so severely that Dad had it demolished, salvaging as much as possible. Those setbacks along with a change in sport fishing habits (sport fishermen were now fishing in the ocean more than the river) pretty much shut down the business. As the folks grew older and needed more assistance in maintaining the property, they realized they needed to hire some help and placed an ad in the local paper. A young couple, Laura Higgins and Gair Walker answered the ad and moved into the "little house" as we now called the old mess hall. They proved to be a great help to Mom and Dad and stayed on for several years.

In 1979, Larry Weathers, who was with the Pacific County Historical Museum, approached Mom and Dad about nominating the Station to the National Historic Register. They enthusiastically gave him the go-ahead, and in 1980 that status was achieved. My folks continued to enjoy their lovely, historic home and grounds until Dad's death in 1988.

NATIONAL REGISTER OF HISTORIC PLACES

Washington State Advisory Council on Historic Preservation
and
United States Department of the Interior

In recognition of its significance to our cultural heritage,
the
COLUMBIA RIVER QUARANTINE STATION
in
Knappton vicinity
has been entered in the National Register of Historic Places.
Date Entered: February 8, 1980

House Before Remodel

2001

The Bell's Retirement Home After Being
Moved Back from Highway

Wedding Day at Knappton Cove for
Rex & Nancy Anderson ~ 1962

STORM DAMAGE TO DOCK ~ 1970's

Rex Anderson, Ellen Magette,
Nancy Anderson
Note Remains of Wharf
Building in Background.

Aerial Shot Showing Highway 401 &
Dock Salvage Operation ~ 1975
Pilot Rex Anderson

THE SUBDIVISION FROM HELL

After Dad's death, Mom moved into a retirement center. It was around this time that I began reflecting on the historical significance of the old Station. The site, after all, was on the National Register of Historic Places, the old buildings on shore remained intact and many of the old artifacts were still there. It seemed to me that some preservation of this history was important and the building best suited for a 'museum' was the old quarantine hospital building (aka *The Pesthouse*) – an artifact in itself.

Mom decided she needed to sell the place, but she favored the idea of preserving the history of the old Station. So in order to make it affordable for family members to purchase, she opted to subdivide the property into three lots. My portion was to be the old hospital building where I could go ahead with my 'museum' plans. My brother Tom was to have the middle portion with the old Mess Hall, and my brother Bob's daughter and her husband agreed to buy the eastern section.

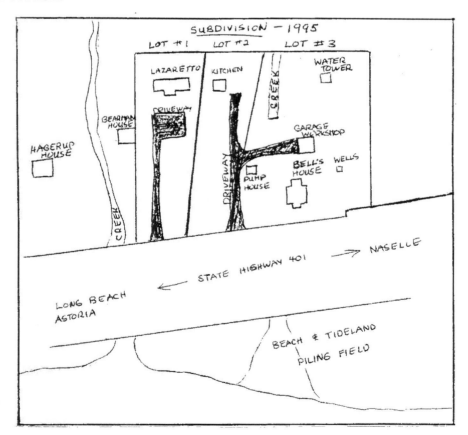

Mom and I went to the County Courthouse to 'do the deed.' What a surprise! Boy, were we naive. It's a good thing we didn't have an inkling of what we were getting into, or it never would have happened. We were thrown into a world of surveyors, engineers and lawyers, endless permits, 2 new septic systems, 2 wells – as well as a good amount of family discord. Suffice it to say, that almost 2 years and $20,000 later the land was indeed divided into three portions looking absolutely no different than when we had started. But, of course, the taxes went up immediately because we now had three taxable lots. And since the subdivision, the taxes on our portion have nearly doubled.

Now I was faced with the hard truth. I had to come up with money to at least make the payments to Mom, pay the taxes, electric bill, and provide for some minimum upkeep. Kind of difficult with a Free Museum. Establishing the Knappton Cove Heritage in 1995, I was convinced that we would be able to provide field trips for school kids – who would pay a modest amount per child. I utilized my background as an elementary teacher and formulated a lesson plan appropriate for third through fifth grades. Armed with the Field Trip Brochure, I visited schools in three counties – with very little success. Only a few classes came. Fortunately, my free-lance craft design work helped toward paying the bills as did occasional renting out of the west wing of the building as a vacation rental apartment, which we named *The Pesthouse Guesthouse*. The debt to my mother was paid off in September of 1999.

KNAPPTON COVE HERITAGE CENTER
ESTABLISHED 1995

Lazaretto (Hospital Building) *The Pesthouse*
Columbia River Quarantine Station 1899-1938

SCHOOL FIELD TRIPS

Students explore history where it happened!

The People of Knappton Cove

Bottle Rubbing

Educational Themes:
Chinook Indians • Maritime Explorers • Lewis & Clark
Donation Land Claim Settlers • Immigrants • Cannery Workers
Archaeology • Quarantine! • Sport Fishing

THE CLOTHESPIN CONNECTION

One of my more lucrative hobbies (well, sort of) is making original dolls from old-fashioned wooden clothespins and selling my designs. No kidding. I sold hundreds of my designs – mostly clothespin characters – for over 20 years to craft magazines and craft book publishers. During that time, I became hooked on clothespins and started collecting them. My collection was outgrowing our home at about the same time the

Knappton Cove Heritage Center was established, so it was moved to one of the small isolation rooms dubbed "*It's A Small World – the Clothespin Museum.*" As our museum exhibits expanded, it was decided to move the Clothespin Museum out of the Pesthouse and into its own little special building nearby.

In order to relate clothespins to the 'Pesthouse' museum, our daughter and I set up an historical 300-year diorama depicting human activity at Knappton Cove – peopled with clothespin dolls. Our grandkids have also added to our exhibit.

Since people of all nationalities were immigrating to the U.S. and coming through America's ports-of-entry, the possibilities for dolls are endless. That led

us to begin a project we named the "*100,000 Clothespin People Project.*" That is approximately the number of people who passed through health inspection at this Port of Entry between 1899 and 1938. It is our goal for

kids as well as adults to make a clothespin doll reflecting their own heritage and either sending us a picture or the actual doll to display.

16

Then there is a small link to maritime history. Sailors, of course, have dirty clothing. Pictures of early sailing ships show laundered clothes hung out on

Sailing Ship Roxburg at Station– 1902

Photo Courtesy of Columbia River Maritime Museum

the rigging to dry. And early Nantucket sailors, during lulls at sea, carved beautiful clothespins from whalebone. Those clothespins were treasured by their wives and sweethearts because they were so smooth they didn't snag even the most delicate of fabrics.

(Vintage Toy Clothespin Sailor, Researched & Reproduced by Nancy Bell Anderson)

Our daughter has joined me in forming a Mother-Daughter team that loves to explore our heritage through crafting. We enjoy our journey into the past, into a time when toys and dolls were made with simple and readily available household items as well as

'treasures' from nature: acorns and their caps, twigs, moss, maple 'wings,' etc.... Of course, we are especially fond of old-fashioned clothespins which show up in most of our kits and publications. We sell our kits, patterns, books and dolls in our "Clothespin Museum & Gift Shop" as well as in other museums. You can check out our website: www.heritagefolk.com. We often refer to our heritage preservation project as the *'museum that clothespins built.'* The sale of those early clothespin designs certainly initially contributed financially to keeping this historic preservation dream afloat.

Popular Heritage Folk Kits

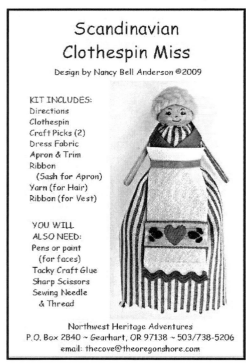

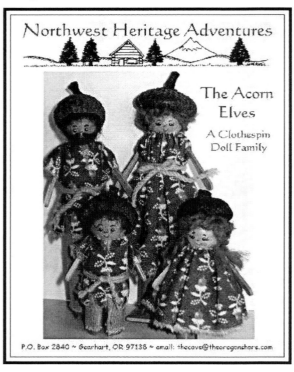

Other Popular Kits Include Peg Leg Pete, Pioneer Dolly, Japanese Lady, Chinook Indians, Indian Brave, Sacajawea's Papoose, Sunflower & Autumn Leaf Fairies along with our pattern books.

A LOOK BACK IN TIME

As our museum project began to evolve, we embarked on a trip back in time. This seemingly isolated spot emerged as a fascinating time capsule. The earliest recorded history dates to 1792, but there is evidence and oral history that pinpoints what is now Knappton Cove as being inhabited by the Chinook Indians as a temporary camping and fishing site for perhaps hundreds, even thousands of years. The protected cove and deep channel were a draw. Indeed, this site has historically attracted human activity and presents a microcosm of American history, specifically Pacific NW history. The land tells the story of our past from the American Indians, the early maritime explorers, the fur traders and the Lewis & Clark Expedition, to the pioneers who settled in the Northwest, and the thousands of immigrants who came attracted by the salmon and timber industries.

1858 Drawing by James Swan Entitled **"Salmon Fishing at Chenook"**
Showing Indians Pulling in Fishing Nets

Our recorded story begins in May of 1792 when the American Captain Robert Gray sailed his ship the *Columbia Rediviva* into the mouth of this great river. Earlier explorations of the Pacific coast by Captain James Cook in his ship the *Endeavor* had opened up the lucrative fur trade, but the fabled large river eluded them. In 1778 John Ledyard, who sailed with Cook, published a journal telling of the riches to be found in the fur trade along the north Pacific coast.

19

After reading the journal a Boston merchant, Joseph Burrell along with 5 partners, sent Captain Gray to Nootka Sound. There they bartered with the Indians for furs which they took to China and sold at a terrific profit. Of course, this spurred on a second trip to the Northwest. It was also Ledyard's writings that, several years later, greatly influenced Thomas Jefferson's decision to send Lewis & Clark on their expedition of discovery.

It was on this second voyage that Captain Gray ventured across the bar and entered the Columbia River. According to Carlton Appelo's book **Knappton, The First 50 Years,** Gray's fur gathering expedition anchored off Point Ellice and then proceeded upstream to Portuguese Point. He then returned to the vicinity of Knappton Cove. The ship's log for May 15, 1792 states: "Light airs and pleasant weather; many natives from different tribes came alongside... In the afternoon, Captain Gray and Mr. Hoskins, in the jolly boat, went on shore to take a short view of the country." The Indian men were described as "in a state of Nature" and the women as wearing nothing but a woven mat apron.

Five months later, the British brig *Chatham* – part of Captain George Vancouver's fleet – visited the Knappton area under the command of Lieutenant William R. Broughton. It seems that Vancouver had obtained a copy of Gray's sketch of the Columbia River entrance while sailing around the north coast of what is now the state of Washington. At this point in time both the English and Americans were vying for control of the fur trade in the Northwest. Vancouver's

H.M.S. CHATHAM was a "Brig"
A Two-Masted Square-Rigged Vessel
Moored at the Knappton Cove Site
November 1792

ship the *H.M.S. Discovery* was thought to be too large to cross the treacherous bar, so Broughton was instructed to explore the river in the *Chatham.* Edward Bell, the *Chatham's* clerk, described crossing the bar in these words, "We had a very fresh Breeze in our favour, but a Strong tide against us, which over the Shoals raised so very heavy and irregular a Sea, that it made a fair breach over us, and our Jolly Boat which was towing astern, was stove to pieces, and everything in her was lost...I never felt more alarmed & frightened in my life, never having been before in a situation where I conceived there was so much danger." The two ships would meet later in San Francisco. According to Appelo, on October

24th, the ship's log states that three canoes of Indians paid the *Chatham* a visit after it anchored near the future site of the Quarantine Station where they sold a few salmon and made signs that they would come back later.

Thomas Manby, Master's Mate along with a skeleton crew, remained at the Knappton site while Broughton and the rest of his men rowed the cutter 110 miles upriver near present day Washougal, Washington. On this exploration trip he named sites including Point Vancouver and Mt. Hood in order to establish English claim to the country. Broughton was the first to conduct an extensive survey and chart the river. He provided the greatest single increase in geographical knowledge of the Northwest coast as well as the Columbia River in his five years in the area. It's interesting to note that on Vancouver's charts the river is called OREGON rejecting Gray's naming of the river as COLUMBIA. A replica of the cutter was built for the 1992 Maritime Bicentennial Commemorative Event for a reenactment of Broughton's upriver expedition. Cutters were built for the Royal Navy because they were fast and light. They originated in the town of Deal where their best customers were smugglers. The Navy soon acquired cutters of their own in order to catch these outlaws. There is a fine model of the *Chatham* and the cutter, built by Eric Pardy, on display in the Columbia River Maritime Museum in Astoria. Tucked inside the cutter is the ship's launch, a sturdier boat used to carry the ship's anchor and heavy casks. Excellent mixed-media drawings by Hewitt Jackson made in 1966 of both the *Chatham* and the *Columbia Rediviva* are also displayed there.

Appelo goes on to state that Manby was given orders to be watchful of the Indians and replenish stocks of wood and water while Broughton was exploring. He purchased a large canoe from the natives and wrote that, "a party of natives took up residence under a tree abreast the vessel; the men supplied him with fish, and the good natured females came on board daily to get themselves adorned with Beads and Buttons. Indeed, over 200 years later, Rex Anderson (author's husband) kicked over a mole hill while mowing the grass and up popped seven blue trade beads. We think one of those gals must have carelessly dropped them. Those precious beads are now on display in our museum. Manby described the moorage site as follows:

INDIAN TRADE BEADS

FROM MOLE HILL

"All the land near the Ship was of moderate (height) and very woody. The roots of the trees growing close down to the high-water mark; the timber common to De Fuga likewise grew here; and a greater proportion of Ash than was seen on any other part of the Coast. A great deal of driftwood at all times floating with the tide, and served our purpose to complete our stock of Fire-Wood without much trouble. The River at our anchorage was seven miles in breadth, but we could observe it decreased to half that about ten miles farther up; it then took a more S.E. direction but how it trended after that we could not ascertain from the Vessel. In mid-channel the tide run very rapid rising eleven feet perpendicular height at the time of the Spring."

Manby also recorded this about the Chinooks: "Altho' the weather was very cold they wore scarcely any covering, most of the men and boys were naked; the women cover their shoulders with a small skin and wear twisted grass about their middle. The hair of most of them is long, coarse, and black... Both men and women assist in paddling the Canoe. The men hunt and the cooking part falls to the lot of the Ladies. Broiling half through is all the preparation either fish or flesh goes through to prepare it for eating. The men never move without their quivers filled with arrows all of which are stained with various colors and pointed with flint made exceedingly sharp; they seldom miss a mark at twenty yards and will often kill a bird at forty." In all of the written accounts by Europeans, their admiration of the hunting and navigational skills of the Chinooks is evident.

As the new century approached, big changes were looming on the horizon for the Pacific Northwest. The Columbia River, which until then had eluded the early maritime explorers, was destined to become a river of unprecedented commerce. The local Indian tribes had, of course, already established a great deal of trading along the river. The demand for furs was soon to be replaced with an even greater demand for timber and salmon. The abundance of resources seemed endless and the race was on!

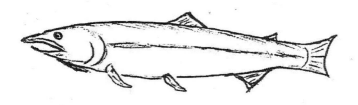

Salmon Sketch by Nancy Bell Anderson

THE LEWIS & CLARK EXPEDITION: NOVEMBER ON THE NORTH SHORE – 1805

Back on the east coast, interest in the west was growing rapidly. President Thomas Jefferson was intensely concerned with stretching the boundaries of the young nation all the way to the Pacific Ocean. He hoped to find a waterway that would to link the Missouri River to the west coast via the Columbia River – a Northwest Passage. So began the training of his young secretary, Meriwether Lewis, to lead an exploratory military expedition up the Missouri to its source in search of this 'passage.' The mission of the expedition would be to reach the Pacific. Dr. Benjamin Rush, the leading physician in the U.S. gave Lewis special medical training. Scores of other experts instructed him on every anticipated aspect of the mission. Plans were already underway when Opportunity knocked, and Jefferson made the risky purchase of the French Imperial province of Louisiana from Napoleon for $12 million in 1803. The whole sale was a bit murky since the territory was occupied by Spain instead of the seller, France! In addition, Jefferson followed this with a secret request to Congress asking for $2,500 to finance the expedition. Because of the Louisiana Purchase, the U.S. was then justified in its exploration efforts of its new acquisition.

The President instructed Lewis, "The object of your mission is to explore the Missouri river & such principal stream of it, as, by its course & communication with the waters of the Pacific Ocean, may offer the most direct & practicable water communication across the continent, for the purposes of commerce." Further instructions were given to study the plant and animal life, make maps and keep written records of their observations. They were also told to make friendly contact with the Indians along the way. Captain Lewis requested that his trusted friend and experienced military officer Captain William Clark be assigned to share his command of this Corps of Discovery. Ultimately, a diverse party was formed: 23 Army privates, 3 sergeants, 2 interpreters, and Clark's African-American slave York. The interpreter Charbonneau's young Shoshone Indian wife, Sacagawea and her infant son also accompanied the party. Captain Lewis's large black Newfoundland dog, Seaman, should also be included.

They departed near the mouth of the Missouri on May 14, 1804. They made winter camp at a Mandan village in North Dakota proceeding on early the following spring. It became apparent that the flow of the Missouri was rapidly decreasing and that the hoped for waterway did not exist – and the Rocky Mountains loomed ahead. But despite their disappointment, they continued on – overcoming incredible difficulties to reach the Columbia River. By October, 1805 there were at last signs that they were nearing their destination – sightings of scarlet & blue cloth, brass tea kettles, a British musket, a cutlass, a sword and seashell ornaments in the pierced noses of the Indians. On November 1 & 2 they made their way through the final barrier on the Columbia— the "Great Shute"— 4 miles of rapids that passed through a series of chutes and falls "the water passing with great velocity forming and boiling in a most horriable manner." But beyond the Great Shute the river widened "and had every appearance of being effected by the tide." At Beacon Rock, they took note of tidal action. They were overjoyed when their overland voyage connected with Captain Broughton's maps as they passed by the Sandy River. Numerous Indian villages began to appear, and they saw the first coastal canoes on November 5 as well as some Indians attired in sailor jackets, shirts and hats. They knew that each mile was bringing them closer to the ocean.

Oregon Grape

On November 7, the expedition reached Pillar Rock, and Clark's journal exclaims, "Great joy in camp we are in view of the Ocian, this great Pacific Octean which we have been so long anxious to See." After their long, difficult journey the Corps of Discovery was on the brink of fulfilling its mission – as directed by President Jefferson – to reach the Pacific. They had several miles yet to go on this great untamed river, but they were getting close! You'll note odd spelling in the quotes from their journals. These were highly intelligent men, but not great spellers. Creative spelling was common at that time. Sometimes several misspellings of the same word occur in the same sentence. The following day they camped on Gray's Bay. On November 9, they apparently camped in the vicinity of Portuguese Point where they were nearly wiped out by floating driftwood, and the storm raged on –"montrous trees, 200 feet long and up to 7

24

feet in diameter." We're talking Old Growth here. "Rained very hard the greater part of the last night & continues this morning, the wind has layed and the swells are fallen. We loaded our canoes and proceed on." On Sunday, November 10 they canoed right past Knappton Cove – hugging the shoreline because of the storm – and made it as far as Hungry Harbor about 1/4 mile downriver from the cove, where they hunkered in for a miserable night.

"The wind rose from the N.W. and the swells became so high, we were compelled to return about 2 miles to a place where we could unld our canoes, which was in a small Bay on Driftwood on which we had also to make our fires to dry our selves as well as we could, the shore being either a clift of Purpendicular rocks or steep assents to the hight of 4 or 500 feet, we continued on this drift wood untill about 3 o'Clock when the evening appearing favourable we loaded & set out in hopes to turn the Point below and get into a better harber, but finding the waves & swells continue to rage with great fury below, we got a safe place for our stores & a much beter one for the canoes to lie and formed a campment on Drift logs in the same little Bay under a high hill at the enterence of a small drean, which we found very convnt. on account of its water, as that of the river is Brackish. The logs on which we lie is all on flote every high tide. The rain continues all day, we are all wet also our bedding and maney other articles, we are all employed untill late drying our bedding, nothing to eate but Pounded fish." Not a pretty picture.

The beach at Knappton Cove is today still strewn with driftwood and at high tide on a stormy day is reminiscent of that November 10 in 1805. Winter storms called *sou'westers* still frequently  batter the area. It is not uncommon for wind gusts to reach over 60 miles per hour. Today power outages occur at such times nearly every winter. But if you're cozy inside by a wood-burning or oil stove, listening to a howling windstorm can be quite exhilarating. It's especially fun if you have a lantern or two, some candles glowing and a wind-gauge to monitor the velocity of the wind.

The expedition managed to make it around Cliff Point at Hungry Harbor. They were again pinned down for several days at Point Ellice. The journal entry

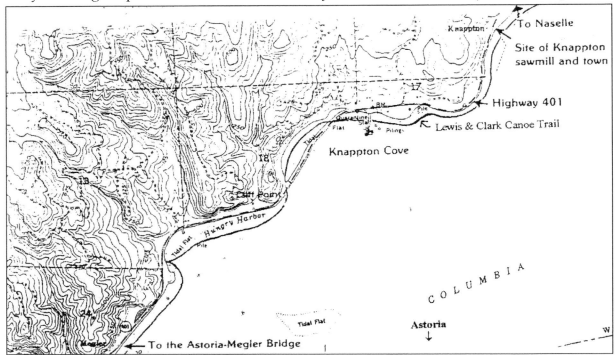

for November 11 records: "A hard rain all the last night, during the last tide the logs on which we lay was all on float, Sent out Jo Fields to hunt, he Soon returned and informed us that the hills was So high & Steep, & thick with undergroth and fallen Timber that he could not get out any distance; about 12 oClock 5 Indians came down in a canoe, the wind verry high from the S.W. with most tremendious waves brakeing with great violence against the Shores, raing

falling in torrents, we are all wet as usial – and our Situation is truly a disagreeable one; the great quantities of rain which has loosened the Stones on the hill Sides; and the Small stones fall down upon us, our canoes at one place at the mercy of the waves, our baggage in another; and our selves and party Scattered on floating logs and Such dry Spots as can be found on the hill sides, and crivicies of the rocks, we purchased of the Indians 13 red charr which we found to be an excellent fish. they are badly clad & illy made, Small and Speak a language much resembling the last nation, one of those men had on a salors Jacket and Pantiloons, and made Signs that he got those clothes from the white people who lived below the point &c. those people left us and crossed the river (which is about 5 miles wide at this place) through the highest waves I ever saw a Small vestles ride. Those Indians are certainly the best Canoe navigators I ever, saw, rained all day." Clark also noted that the women tattooed their legs, wore their hair loose and wore ear ornaments and that both the men and women had flattened heads. The women wore short skirts made from twisted cedar bark attached to a belt and sometimes a short robe. He also writes, "maney of the women are handsom" and that they all went barefooted.

Clark further states: "It would be distressing to a feeling person to See our Situation at this time all wet and cold with our bedding &c. also wet, in a Cove Scercely large enough to Contain us...canoes at the mercy of the waves & driftwood...robes & leather Clothes are rotten. On November 15, a break in the weather finally made it possible to round Point Ellice and a camp was set up at what later became known as McGowan's Landing – the place our family used to camp each summer and fish for salmon. Station Camp – as it was dubbed in their journals – became a temporary headquarters for 10 days. It was at this point that their mission of reaching the Pacific Ocean was accomplished. They were near a Chinook Indian village where they became acquainted with Chief Concomly. He was a very influential figure in the lower Columbia area for many years.

Picture below and on previous page were taken from Interpretive Panels at The Dismal Nitch.

Clark's journal entry states: "this I could plainly See would be the extent of our journey by water, ...in full view of the Ocian from Point Adams...to Cape Disappointment." From Station Camp, they explored the Long Beach peninsula by foot. It was at this camp that it was determined where they should make their winter encampment. By this time, they were in dire straits. Their clothing was rotting and their food supplies nearly depleted. The choices were to stay where they were, go back upriver to the Sandy River area or cross the river where they were told that elk were more abundant. And contact with the friendly Clatsop Indians who had visited from across the river influenced their decision. The Chinooks on the north shore were more experienced at trading and drove a harder bargain, and the expedition's trade goods were becoming very limited. Stormy weather continued to plague them. The November 22 journal entry sums it up appropriately, "before day the wind increased to a storm...and blew with violence throwing the water of the river with emence waves out of its banks almost over whelming us in water, O! how Horriable is the day."

The entire expedition was polled (a bit unusual for the military and even more unusual in that both York and Sacagawea were included), and the decision was made to cross the river so they could replenish their supplies and prepare for the return trip. There was also the hope that they might connect with a ship that could take some of them and their valuable information back to the east coast. They departed from Station Camp on November 25, and once again they canoed upriver past Knappton Cove and Gray's Bay – crossing where the water was less turbulent just east of Pillar Rock. They came back downriver on the south shore, rounded Tongue Point and explored the area going into Young's Bay where they found a good location for a camp on the Lewis & Clark River. The hoped-for arrival of a ship did not happen, but the replenishing of supplies was accomplished at Fort Clatsop. In what is now the town of Seaside, they boiled ocean water to make salt for preserving meat. A replica of their salt cairn marks the site today. Today the reconstructed fort stands as an historically accurate replica maintained by the U.S. National Park System. After wintering at Fort Clatsop their return journey upriver began on March 23, 1806. This amazing and successful exploratory expedition spurred on and further ignited the inevitable westward expansion.

Now Fort Clatsop has been designated "Lewis & Clark National Park" along with two sites on the Washington shore: "Middle Village" and "The Dismal Nitch" which are located just west of Knappton Cove.

"TODD'S BAY" 1814

The following decade brought more early explorers to the lower Columbia area. In 1811, John Jacob Astor's Pacific Fur Trading Company was established as the first permanent U.S. commercial settlement on the Pacific Coast and named Astoria. But in 1913 John McDonald arrived on the British Sloop of War, *Raccoon* and without much effort took possession of Astoria from the skeleton band of pretty much disinterested Americans. The British flag was hoisted, and the name changed to Fort George.

Now accompanying the *Raccoon* was a supply ship the *Isaac Todd* with Donald McTavish aboard who was assigned to become Governor of this new

outpost. And an entertaining 'Knappton Cove' story unfolds. It seems that back in England before their departure, this assignment loomed as a trip to the ends of the world. So, of course, John and Donald while waiting around for the 'fittings' for their ship visited a pub in Portsmouth for some liquid encouragement. There they met a young barmaid, Jane Barnes, who was described as a lively, flaxen-haired, blue-eyed beauty and evidently Donald was smitten. Jane was persuaded to accompany them on this adventure and was signed on as the ship's seamstress. Jane, however, must have been pretty 'street smart' as we call it today. She said that she would require a goodly supply of silks and plumes and other garments, plus "bottled porter," "excellent cheese," and prime tinned English beef. She must have been exceedingly successful in her requests because the British Navy sent three extra escort vessels along!

The *Isaac Todd* wintered over in San Francisco to spare the passengers the harsh seasonal Pacific NW weather while the *Raccoon* sailed north to establish British claim. While waiting out the winter, they were also involved with purchasing two heifers and two bulls which became the start of the dairy industry in the lower Columbia area. I would imagine that Jane relished this stopover in San Francisco. All told it took 13 months for the *Isaac Todd* to reach Fort George.

Needless to say, Jane – the first white woman to visit the lower Columbia River – caused quite a stir, not only among the men stationed at Fort George, but the Indians as well. According to an account written by Ross Cox who was stationed at Fort George, "The Indians thronged in numbers to our fort for the mere purpose of gazing on, and admiring the fair beauty, every

article of whose dress was examined with the most minute scrutiny. She had rather an extravagant wardrobe, and each day exhibited her in a new dress, which she always managed in a manner to display her figure to the best advantage. One day, her head, decorated with feathers and flowers produced the greatest surprise; the next, her hair, braided and unconcealed by any covering, excited equal wonder and admiration. The young women felt almost afraid to approach her, and the old were highly gratified at being permitted to touch her person." Those silks and plumes were being put to good use on her daily walks along the waterfront! All this proved too much for the spectators, so it was decided that Jane should be sent across to the north side of the river so the men could concentrate on business. And that place was Knappton Cove, where she lived aboard ship. Consequently on maps of that era, and even on the later property description of the donation land claim, the cove was dubbed **Todd's Bay**.

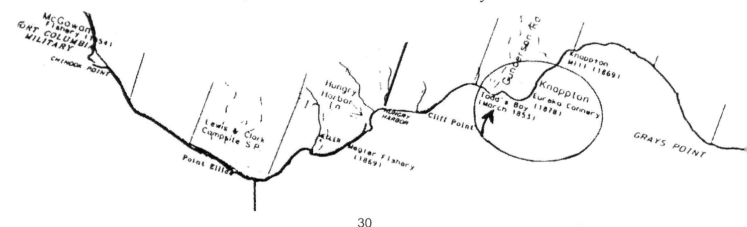

But the story continues. On one of those dark and stormy nights, Donald McTavish along with his clerk and chaperon Alexander Henry and a small crew of six men took off to visit Jane. Their boat capsized and all but one drowned. Donald McTavish's headstone is now on display at the Clatsop County Historical Museum – reportedly the oldest headstone in the Northwest. Ross Cox's book published in 1831 states, "in a handsome spot behind the NE bastion of Fort George...a small monument, tolerably well engraved, points to the future Indian trader the last earthly remains of the enterprising Donald M'Tavish."

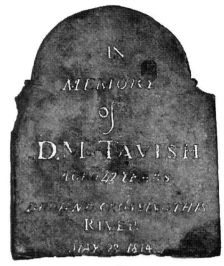

IN
MEMORY
of
D.M'TAVISH
AGED 42 YEARS
DROWND CROSSING THIS
RIVER
MAY 22, 1814

So that left Jane high and dry, so to speak. She did receive an offer by Chief Concomly's son, Cassakas – 100 otter skins (valued at about $100 each – quite a sum at that time) plus a life of ease as his wife. In Don Marshall's book **OREGON SHIPWRECKS** he states, "Jane would not have to cut wood, gather wood, build fires or fetch water." She would have all the tobacco she desired as well as the finest cuts of fish and meat. There were a few catches. He already had four other wives, but he assured her that she would be NUMBER ONE. Big Deal. In essence, Jane said to herself something to the effect of "No way, Jose!" and diplomatically refused the generous offer.

She then shipped out to Canton, China in September 1814 most likely on the brig *Columbia*. Captain Robert Gray's friend, Captain Robson presented a bill for 717 pounds sterling for the "expenses of the female." There appear to be two possible scenarios to the end of this tale. One is that in 1818 Jane returned to Astoria a respectable married woman and mother of two as the wife of Captain Robson. But I think the more plausible one is that she consorted with the head of the East India Company and returned to England, having successfully circumnavigated the globe. To support this theory, there was a Jane Barnes who put in an unsuccessful claim for back wages from the North West Company as an official member of the Fort George expedition back in Portsmouth. She had, after all, been the ship's official seamstress! Now, doesn't that seem more likely for our flamboyant Jane?

Job Lamley's Donation Land Claim 1853-1870

After 1814 there were occasional visits by 'tourists,' and the local Indians migratory trips for food supplies continued in the Knappton Cove area. Then on November 3, 1853 a Donation Land Claim was filed by Job Lamley in Oregon City. It read: "I, Job Lamley of Pacific County in that part of the Territory of Oregon now established as the Territory of Washington hereby give notice of my claim to a portion of 320 acres of land particularly bounded and described as follows: Beginning at this S.W. corner at a Fir Tree one foot in diameter marked Todd's Bay (Remember Jane and the *Isaac Todd*?), Columbia River, Thence 53 E.3.50 chns., N.52 E., 2.50 chns."

Job Lamley

Photo Courtesy of Carlton Appelo

Job Lamley was born in Worcestershire, England in 1829. When he was a youngster his parents immigrated to the U.S. settling in Richland County, Ohio. At age 18 he fought in the Mexican War in 1847 under General Price in the Santa Fe Battalion. He was sent by the government to carry Army supplies across the Plains in the spring of 1849, arriving in Oregon City in November 1849. Lured by the prospect of gold in California, he took passage on the sailing brig, *Josephine*, outbound for San Francisco from Astoria. It was shipwrecked on the notorious Columbia River bar on December 14, 1849. The young adventurer survived, dragging ashore at Baker's Bay (Ilwaco) and joined a group led by Dr. Elijah White. These entrepreneurs determined to found Pacific City – hoping to establish a rival to San Francisco. He made a living at that time fishing but soon turned to politics. He was elected the first sheriff of Pacific County in June, 1852, receiving 16 votes. He was also appointed Pacific County Assessor and served two years in each office.

He resided first in the Deep River area and then in Chinookville where he fell in love with Sarah Frances Wilson – the young daughter of Daniel "Cougar" Wilson. She was also the third cousin of President Woodrow Wilson and had actually become acquainted with Job in Springfield, Illinois when she was a child of 6. She crossed the Plains with her parents in 1849. The young pioneer couple married in 1857 and built a beautiful, stately home complete with an orchard at

Lamley House at Knappton Cove

Photos Courtesy of Seaside Museum & Columbia River Maritime Museum

Todd's Bay (Knappton Cove). Lamley was also instrumental in getting a road built from Naselle to Knappton. Remains of the old orchard remain today and still bear fruit. Job, a sea-faring man often served as a pilot on the Columbia River bar – the same treacherous bar on which he'd been shipwrecked. Sarah bore 9 children, the oldest of whom, Job H. Lamley, Jr. became a well-known riverboat captain on the Columbia. The 1870 census shows that they also employed a 20-year old Chinese day laborer, Chan Charley.

J.B. KNAPP

Jabez Burrell Knapp was born in Ohio August 2, 1821. His family was of German origin. As a young man, Knapp was a teacher in Mississippi and Louisiana for 8 years. He married a southern girl, Miss Lucy Wells. In 1852, he caught 'Oregon Fever.' On the trip westward, both his wife and one of their young daughters died of cholera. He also came close to death, but survived and was able to bring his other daughter overland as far as The Dalles where he then continued to Portland on the steamer, *Multnomah*.

Practically destitute by this time, he located a friend to watch his young daughter and began to hunt for odd jobs. He cut cordwood, made shingles and did a little farming on Sauvie's Island. Then he did some carpentry work. In 1855 he enlisted in the Rogue River Indian War where he served in the Quartermaster Department for about a year. There were nine companies of mounted cavalry in this war which started because of the anger of the Klickitats who had been forcibly relocated and also local Indians who objected to gold prospectors invading their land.

When he was discharged in 1856, he was hired by W.C. Hull, who operated a produce business, as a traveling representative in California for agricultural products. His pay was $100 per month plus expenses. He enjoyed some success and invested his earnings by establishing two orchards in California. In 1857 he went into business with Hull as Hull, Knapp & Co. and cleared $7,500 – a considerable sum at that time. In October 1859 he married Miss Caroline H. Benjamin in Sacramento. Knapp operated their San Francisco office where he received fruit sent down by Oregon farmers. By 1869 he opened a large double fronted store and was receiving up to 9,000 boxes of fruit on each arriving passenger ship from Oregon. But Mr. Hull was contracting large amounts of fruit at fixed prices and the speculation backfired resulting in financial ruin. The partnership was dissolved.

FOUNDER OF KNAPP, BURRELL & CO.

Jabez B. Knapp

Knapp had developed important business connections during his time in San Francisco. So in 1860 he decided to form a new partnership with his cousin Martin Strong Burrell in Portland. Their company – Knapp, Burrell & Co. — became well-known and involved in many business activities. About this time he began exploring the area at the mouth of the Columbia River where his parents and grandparents had settled. In 1867 he discovered boulders along the shore of the bay which he thought would make a fine grade of water cement. So he purchased the east portion of Lamley's land claim. In 1869 he and his wife Caroline built a home near the Lamley's and later took up residence there. In 1870 he removed himself from the Portland firm. That same year his son J.B. Jr. was born. A ledge of rock just upriver from Todd's Bay became the basis for his new venture. Job Lamley along with J.H. Burl and George T. Hopkins joined him. There they built a large kiln and barrel factory to handle the production from the cement business and established Cementville. But the raw material soon began to give out and the cement operation was shut down in a few short years.

Evidently realizing that the cement factory was going to be temporary, Knapp organized the Columbia River Manufacturing Co. and started a sawmill business. The town's name was changed to Knappton. The sawmill began operating in 1870 even while the cement plant was still in operation. The 1870 census showed a population of 112 at Knappton. There was also a schoolhouse and boarding house listed. There were 29 dwellings. In 1871 a post office was established there. The cement plant buildings eventually became a store and a dance hall.

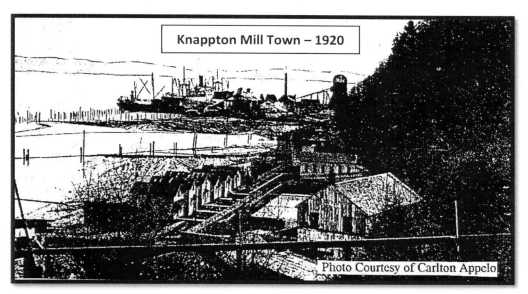

Knappton Mill Town – 1920

Photo Courtesy of Carlton Appelo

Knapp continued to operate the mill until the fall of 1876 when the he sold out to Captain Asa E. Simpson and the Knapps moved to the Vancouver area. This resilient gentleman was described in his obituary in 1900 as kind-hearted, genial, well known and highly respected. Knappton was a bustling, thriving mill town well into the 1930's and has been well documented in Carlton Appelo's book **Knappton, The First 50 Years.** Sadly, a major fire along with flooding devastated the little town and all that remains today is a sizable piling field – more than a thousand! Knappton is just one of many ghost towns along the banks of the Columbia leaving only those silent piling as testimonials to these once thriving river communities.

EUREKA & EPICURE PACKING COMPANY 1876-1897

The remaining western portion of Lamley's Donation Land Claim was sold in 1876 to Joseph Hume for a cannery. The Hume family (descendants of King Kenneth II) had immigrated to America from Scotland in 1793 and originally settled near the Kennebec River in Maine. There they had a friend, Andrew Hapgood, who had been experimenting with canning lobsters. Joseph was the youngest of four brothers who came west and began canning salmon at Sacramento in 1864. Until this time there was no other way of preserving the great abundance of salmon except by drying, smoking or packing in salt brine. The large barrels of salted salmon frequently spoiled. So the brothers invited Hapgood and his canning equipment to join them in California and started canning the salmon. Canned salmon was an immediate success. The Hume Brothers built the first salmon cannery on the Columbia in 1867 at Eagle Cliff in Wahkiakum County. They continued building canneries on both sides of the river from Astoria to Longview. By 1881, the four Hume brothers (William, George W., Robert D. and Joseph) had built more than half of the canneries on the Columbia. Their enormous success spurred on others – peaking in 1883 at 39 canneries on the Columbia.

Many Chinese immigrants began arriving here in the 1850's, first to clear the land for wheat farms and then to work for the railroads. When George Hume began having difficulty with his cannery workers, his Chinese cook suggested that he hire Chinese workers. George became the first to employ Chinese laborers in his canneries in 1870. They found them to be dependable, good, steady workers. Many could clean a 40- pound salmon in 45 seconds amounting to 1700 fish in an eleven hour day. They were paid $180 to $200 per season, which was about the same as the gillnetters were getting. In 1880 there were

4,000 Chinese in the lower Columbia area. The 1880 census showed 18 Chinese working at the Knappton mill plus 3 cooks and 70 Chinese employed at Joseph Hume's cannery at Knappton Cove.

Picture taken from Ship's Crow's Nest

Chinese Pottery Shards Found on Site

Photo Courtesy of Columbia River Maritime Museum

Joseph Hume's Eureka & Epicure Packing Company
1876-1890's

Hume's **EUREKA & EPICURE PACKING COMPANY** was licensed in both Oregon and Washington. His first brand name was **STAR,** then became **BEACON.**

He claimed his salmon were the freshest and highest quality because he could actually see the fish being caught right in front of his cannery docks. He demanded that the fish be cooked slowly since, "too rapid cooking renders it strong, rancid, and unwholesome." One of the original labels pictures details that are amazing, amusing and prophetic! Lady Liberty lifts high a salmon 'torch' and clutches a large Costco-sized can of salmon in the other hand. That was two decades before the Port of Astoria had its own version of "Ellis Island." The label also shows a bridge and city in the background, obviously New York, but looks very much like today's Astoria/Megler bridge and the city of Astoria.

The first boats in Hume's employ were the "Butterfly Fleet" – so called because with all their sails furled, they resembled butterflies flitting across the river. Unfortunately, there was a great deal of prejudice against the Chinese. Americans of European descent regarded them with suspicion because of the big differences in cultural practices.

Chinese wore pajama-like *sahms*, spoke in a singsong like manner and ate very different kinds of food. The men wore their hair in long braided queues and their religion was alien to the Caucasians. So they were relegated to the least desirable jobs available and often treated despicably. Coolies (meaning "bitter labor") were brought to America in holds of ships as cargo, much like the black slaves from Africa. Employers paid about $100 for each man's passage, and he then became indentured in order to work off his debt. By the 1870's immigrants from many other countries, lured by the burgeoning salmon and timber industries, were also flowing into the region. A hierarchy quickly developed. The Chinese were allowed only to work in the canneries and never permitted to fish commercially. Indeed, it was said, "Any Chinaman caught fishing was a dead Chinaman." Sadly, there actually were brutal killings of Chinese caught fishing. Commercial

fishing was done by the European immigrants – most of whom came from the Nordic countries where their families had fished for generations. By 1876 there was a depression and American laborers wanted even the lowly jobs held by the Chinese. In 1882 Congress passed the first of three Exclusion Acts, which

forbade most Chinese from entering the U.S. And by around 1900 a mechanical device was invented that beheaded and cleaned salmon. The machine was dubbed the derogatory term 'the Iron Chink' because it replaced Chinese labor.

Today!
The Model G "Iron Chink"
A complete Salmon Butchering and Slicing Machine which represents the utmost in raw material and labor saving equipment.

Smith Cannery Machines Co.
Seattle, Wash.

Even as early as the mid 1870's the market for canned salmon was becoming glutted. Consequently, profits began to decline. So in 1882 Hume sold his cannery to the KNAPPTON PACKING COMPANY, which later became the COLUMBIA RIVER PACKING ASSOCIATION (CRPA). This group, known as the 'Combine,' was headquartered in Astoria. The Combine stabilized the industry by closing or consolidating canneries. The cannery at Knappton Cove was closed and put up for sale.

MAKES A CANNERY PAY WITHOUT CHINESE

J. O. Morris, manager of the Everett Packing company, who is well known in Hoquiam where he formerly lived, is here with Mrs. Morris for a few days' visit. "Our company demonstrated during its first season's operations that salmon can be packed at a profit without the aid of Oriental labor," said Mr. Morris yesterday. "The capacity of our plant is 3000 cases a day; our entire pack of 65,000 cases was sold early and we have an order for 20,000 cases of this year's pack from a St. Louis firm to whom we shipped three carloads last season."

Because Chinese were not permitted in Everett, Mr. Morris and associates were told by packers of the Northwest that they couldn't make their plant pay. "But we did make it pay," he continued. "It not only paid us but was a good thing for the town. We employed 165 persons at the height of the salmon season, and many of these were high school girls and boys who made from $2.50 to $4.50 a day, and all of that money went into circulation at home."

The company made the use of Orientals unnecessary by introducing the sanitary automatic system of canning, which dispenses with hand soldering.

Daily Washington -- Hoquiam 1914

Current PHS
Service Emblem

THE COLUMBIA RIVER'S *"ELLIS ISLAND"* 1899-1938
U.S. GOVERNMENT QUARANTINE STATION

By the turn of the century, due to difficult times abroad, immigration had greatly increased and with it came health concerns. So now for a little background, once again we dip back in time. In the 1800's infectious disease had been a serious problem, and much of it was spread by the shipping industry. Early sailing ships were often notoriously unclean and infested with rats. The fleas on the rats were the carriers of the dreaded bubonic plague or 'black death.' Smallpox, yellow fever, cholera and typhoid were also prevalent. There already existed an Anglo-American tradition of public health provision for mariners dating to the 16th century. A hospital was built for members of the Royal Navy, and various sailor welfare systems were instigated in both the colonies of North Carolina and Virginia.

So in 1798, our 5th Congress enacted legislation signed by President John Adams establishing a Marine Hospital Fund under the Treasury Department. Our young nation was dependent upon the sea for both trade and protection. This law would encourage expansion of the existing, small merchant marine and "provide for the accommodation of sick and disabled seamen." At that time, the arrival of ill sailors in our ports placed a burden on our public hospitals. Furthermore, these unattached seamen were often unkempt and downright dirty which proved offensive to hospital staff and regular patients. Twenty cents a month was deducted from the seamen's wages to finance the Fund – indeed, our first managed health care system. So began what today we know as the U.S. Public Health Service (USPHS).

Marine hospitals were first established along the Eastern seaboard and then along inland routes of shipping and commerce including New Orleans, St. Louis and Paducah, Kentucky. As exploration and settlement opened up the West, a hospital was built in San Francisco. Misuse and corruption began to get a foothold in the operation and establishment of these facilities. During the Civil War both Union and Confederate armies freely occupied these hospitals for their own use. After the war, only eight of the original 27 hospitals were operational. And a Wisconsin senator, Timothy Otis Howe stated: "A favorite way of starting a town in the West, if it was anywhere on a stream or on a goodsized puddle, was to get an appropriation for a marine hospital." Reports critical of the Marine Hospital Fund as disorganized, irregular and subject to local patronage led to a reform act in 1870.

Earlier Service Emblem, before 1902

This act organized the marine hospitals into a centrally controlled system headed by a "Supervising Surgeon." Dr. John Woodworth was appointed to the post in April 1871. He reorganized the Service along military lines. Local physicians were replaced with medical officers who were admitted only after examination and were subject to assignment wherever required. In 1889 Congress officially established the Marine Hospital Service (MHS) Commissioned Corps with uniforms and ranks modeled after the military. Titles and pay corresponded with Army and Navy grades. Dr. Woodworth's title became "Supervising Surgeon General" and finally in 1902 "Surgeon General." His reports carried the fouled anchor, representing sick and disabled seamen and the caduceus of Mercury, seal of the Service, symbolizing maritime commerce. That seal with a two-winged staff entwined by two snakes or serpents is still used by the Public Health Service. In fact, it is often used in place of the real medical symbol – the caduceus of Aesculapius (es ku-la pe-us), the Greek

Rubbing from bottle at Station: "Public Health and Marine Hospital Service" dates bottle to Service Emblem used 1902-1912.

God of Medicine – which is just one staff and one snake. The serpent, which sheds its skin yearly as well as the healing power of its venom, symbolizes the renewal of life. At right, are two versions of the *REAL* medical symbol, though not as familiar caduceus of Mercury.

The PHS has two official flags. The Surgeon General's flag consists of the Service corps device in white on a field of blue. Any commissioned quarantine vessel must fly that flag from the foremast during the Surgeon General's stay on board the vessel. If the vessel does not have a mast, the flag is flown at the jack staff. The quarantine flag is the same as the Surgeon General's except the PHS corps device is blue on a yellow field. It is flown at quarantine stations and on a quarantine vessel from the jack staff, except when the vessel has no mast and the presence of the Surgeon General necessitates the use of that staff for his personal flag. Blue stands for the care of merchant seamen and yellow signifies maritime quarantine functions.

The international signal flag for quarantine is a 2'x2' yellow flag. Signal flags are made of a heavy material, and there are flags for each letter of the alphabet. A ship flying one "Q" flag signifies "Request for Pratique" or "Quarantine Inspection Required." "Pratique" is defined in Webster's Dictionary as "clearance given an incoming ship by the health authority of a port." If a ship flies one "Q" flag over another, it indicates "Ship in Quarantine, Illness on Board."

By 1878 the Marine Hospital Service began to take on more public health issues. The spread of disease was a serious problem. Mosquitoes carried yellow fever, and lice spread typhus. Bubonic plague was spread by fleas living on infected rats that infested the ships. Ship captains were warned:

Rats carry plague, mosquitoes carry yellow fever
Plague and yellow fever cause quarantine
Quarantine means expense
Ship captains, destroy your rats and mosquitoes, and not only
    save your owners money, but save lives.

The word 'quarantine' comes from an Italian word 'quarantina' meaning 'forty.' Originally it meant forty days of isolation required for a ship arriving from a foreign port that was known to have epidemic diseases. International quarantine originated in the 14th century, most likely in Venice. Special areas in harbors were set aside for quarantine. To this day, ports have quarantine areas in which ships suspect to disease must remain, have no contact with land, and fly the yellow "Q" signal flag (indicating quarantine) until official permission to proceed is granted.

In 1889 Congress enacted a national quarantine law to prevent the introduction of contagious diseases into the United States. Federal legislation in 1891 mandated the inspection of all arriving immigrants and assigned this task to the MHS. The law stipulated the exclusion of "all idiots, insane persons, paupers or persons likely to become public charges, persons suffering from a loathsome or dangerous contagious disease and criminals" – not a bad idea. Immigrants were coming to the U.S. by the thousands each week. Although Ellis Island (which opened in 1892) handled the largest numbers, there were many other U.S. ports of entry.

Health concerns prompted the residents of the lower Columbia River to demand a quarantine station and hospital. Astoria had a public health inspector but ships with disease found on board had to be sent 275 miles north to Port Townsend for fumigation. Of course, this was not good for business! Both Oregon and Washington Congressmen recommended a disinfecting facility at an estimated cost of $40,000, but the request was denied. Finally, in 1897, Senator McBride of Oregon introduced another similar bill and in 1898 a 3-man committee was chosen to investigate possible sites near Astoria. When they heard about the selection committee, the Astorians got a bad case of *NIMBY* (not-in-my-backyard). So the search went across the river, as well. Astorians thought the deserted cannery near Knappton on the other side of the river would do nicely. The deep channel, existing wharf buildings, and sparse population in the immediate area were pluses. The committee decided the Knappton site was ideal.

The residents in Washington were not overjoyed. Their Senator John L. Wilson received a letter from M.P. Callender, President of the North Pacific Improvement Company at

Knappton which stated: "The citizens of Astoria, Oregon, and places contiguous, by persistent petitioning of Congress, secured appropriation for the establishing of a quarantine station at that port. A commission was appointed to select a site for such a station. In pursuit of their duties they were met at every turn with opposition by the Oregon residents to the location of such station anywhere in their immediate vicinity...they were compelled to come to the north side of the Columbia ... Finding at this place a small piece of land owned by Astorians...the Commission selected this as a site for the station, and against the wishes and protests of the people for whom I petition. This company was formed for the purpose of developing and improving the country along the north side of the Columbia by building a railroad and finally a city...Now, this site for a quarantine station is in the very heart of the proposed town site and projected improvements, and, if finally established there, will utterly annihilate the capital invested and render valueless the holdings of this company...this wrong is to be done to your constituents and the State of Washington at the behest of, and for the advantage of, residents of Oregon, people who are ever clamoring for government appropriations and institutions, and when secured are unwilling to give space for their establishment." So there!

But despite this outcry, negotiations were completed in 1899, and the site was purchased by the government for $8,000. The Columbia River Quarantine Station was established by Assistant Surgeon Hill Hastings on May 9, 1899. The new disinfecting building on the wharf was completed in 1900. Hastings was soon replaced by Assistant Surgeon Baylis H. Earle who assumed command of

Street Scene in Astoria Showing Marine Hospital Service Sign

Photo Courtesy of Columbia River Maritime Museum

the station on December 12, 1900. The main offices of the Marine Hospital Service were located in Astoria in the Spexarth Building. Later the offices were located on the second floor of the Scandinavian American Bank on 10th Street. Rent for the two rooms there in 1915 was $20 per month. Ships crossing the Columbia bar first anchored at the port of Astoria where an inspector boarded and checked for infestation and communicable disease.

Health Guardians at the Gate c. 1906
Columbia River Quarantine Station Personnel

Back row from left to right: Frank Williams, Joe Johnson, Thad Trullinger, Capt. Babbidge, Unknown, Ole Estoos, Johnnie Lindberg, and Johnnie Smith. Front row: Madge Sovey, Assistant Surgeon Dr. Baylis H. Earle (in charge of the station at the time), and Annie Abraham. Dr. Earle lived in Astoria, but he made frequent trips to Knappton Cove to hold muster and fire drills and inspect ships when there were at the wharf.

If deemed necessary, the ship was then immediately sent over to Knappton Cove for fumigation. An article by DeWitt Harry in the October 2, 1921 Oregonian stated: "Pratique is granted foreign vessels entering the Columbia River at Astoria, which ranks as one of the main points of entry and clearance for offshore traffic in America. ... Before any vessel coming from a foreign port can discharge or load cargo in the Columbia River it must pass quarantine at Astoria. The 'Ellis Island' for this district is situated on the Washington side of the river, near Knappton; and consists of a dock, disinfecting building and appliances, quarters, hospital, detention quarters, etc. ... Thanks to the vigilance of the quarantine on the Columbia river our cities have yet to experience the plague."

The incoming vessel was moored at the east end of the dock where passengers and crew disembarked. Inside the dock building they stripped, took

U.S.S. Concord

showers, and went through health inspection while their luggage and clothing were deloused in huge retorts. The retorts from the old cannery were converted to handle the disinfecting. If they passed health inspection, they bunked ashore in tents. In April of 1915 more comfortable accommodations were provided aboard the *U.S.S. Concord,* which was moored at the west end of the dock. The ship had been decommissioned from the Spanish-American War and put into use as a temporary lodging place.

The arriving vessel was sealed off, and sulfur was burned in large pots placed throughout the ship. The fumes killed the rats and other vermin. Most of the time, this process was uneventful but Harold Hagerup who lived just west of the Station recalled an unfortunate accident in which sulfur fumes infiltrated the shower rooms, causing a hasty exodus. According to Harold, "there were naked Chinamen running all over the place." The fumigation process took 48 hours, considered only a slight inconvenience in the passage. Anyone diseased or suspect to disease was put into isolation and detained.

Eventually in 1912 the quarantine hospital was built on shore for that purpose. Full capacity of the hospital was 20 patients, but it was only equipped for 11. There were 2 large wards, each with a bathroom, accessible by a common front entry. At each end of the building were two isolation wards accessible by separate exterior entrances. A small bathroom separated those rooms. Evidently, sharing the bathroom was not considered a health risk!

THE 'PESTHOUSE' IN 2009

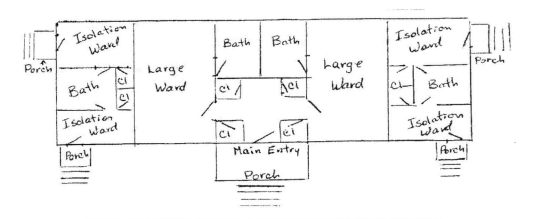

Lazaretto (Pesthouse) Floor Plan
Original Blueprint is On Display in Museum

Physicians and all members of the Commissioned Corps lived in Astoria and visited the Station weekly or more often if a ship was in quarantine. Nurses rarely, if ever, visited the Station. The steamer *Electro* was leased for $260 a month from the Babbidge family of Astoria to serve exclusively as a shuttle between Astoria and the Station. Another steamer, the *Electric* was also one of the shuttle vessels. In 1913 the gasoline launch *Hulda* was chartered for that purpose, replaced by the launch *Donald Currie* around 1922.

> U.S. Public Health Service Personnel on the *Electro* ~ 1905
> The *Electro* was built around 1899 at the Knappton Mill Boat yard where many boats, scows and sailing ships were built for the worldwide lumber trade.

Photo Courtesy of Columbia River Maritime Museum

NO TRESPASSING UNDER PENALTY.
UNITED STATES QUARANTINE STEAMER.
ANY PERSON OR PERSONS
ANTINE STEAMER 'ELEC‗
PERMISSION OF THE MED‗
WILL BE PROSECUTED TO
LAW UNDER ACT OF THE
BOARDING THE U.S. QUAR‗
TRO', EXCEPT BY SPECIAL
ICAL OFFICER IN COMMAND,
THE FULL EXTENT OF THE
CONGRESS OF THE UNITED
STATES OF AUGUST 1, 1888.

Sign from *Electro* now on display in Museum

Captain Babbidge, MHS Owner & Operator of the *Electro.*

Caretakers could live in the house on the station grounds, but since their families were not allowed to live there, they often had homes nearby. The government issued passes to nearby residents so they could enter the property when necessary. The Hagerup family, whose home was just west of the station, walked to school along a boardwalk that traversed the station grounds. When the station was in quarantine, they had to walk on the beach to circumvent the area that was in quarantine. The hospital building was called a 'lazaretto'— an Italian word meaning 'pesthouse' – historically a house for lepers, and later a hospital for those with contagious diseases.

Photos Courtesy of Columbia River Maritime Museum

An excerpt from a 1912 Public Health bulletin found at the Station entitled *A WORD TO SHIP CAPTAINS ABOUT QUARANTINE* states: "...everyone has a horror of catching plague, cholera, yellow fever, smallpox, jail fever, or leprosy. When a

A WORD TO SHIP CAPTAINS ABOUT QUARANTINE.

AN OPEN LETTER TO SHIP CAPTAINS.

By L. E. COFER, Assistant Surgeon General, Chief of the Division of Foreign and Insular Quarantine of the Bureau of the Public Health and Marine-Hospital Service.

There are very few people who would run the risk of plague or yellow fever infection just to save a vessel from being quarantined. No one feels sorry for the expense and trouble put upon the captain and owners of a vessel because of plague or yellow fever being on board. Everyone says "Quarantine it!" and Congress, which represents the will of the people, appropriates a sum of money every year to prevent vessels from infecting ports. Some people object to quarantine, but no one wants it abolished. Why? Because everyone has a horror of catching plague, cholera, yellow fever, smallpox, jail fever, or leprosy. When a person catches any one of these diseases even his friends consider him loathsome (and so he is), and the first thing they say is, "Take him at once to the pesthouse." People have been saying this since biblical times, they are saying it now, and they will keep on saying it. So quarantine is here to stay, and it costs money to operate it, and so far as vessels are concerned, it costs money to run against it. So what is to be done? Well, it is up to you captains of vessels. You can avoid much of the trouble and expense of quarantine for yourselves and also for your owners by following the suggestions made in this little pamphlet. In fact, the whole story is really told in this little table:

NO RATS——NO PLAGUE.

NO MOSQUITOES——NO YELLOW FEVER.

VACCINATE AND——NO SMALLPOX.

PURE FOOD, PURE WATER, AND CLEANLINESS——NO CHOLERA.

NO LICE——NO TYPHUS.

person catches any one of these diseases even his friends consider him loathsome (and so he is) and the first thing they say is, "Take him at once to the pesthouse." The bulletin goes on to describe in gory detail the dreaded plague. The message is, of course, a warning to ship captains to clean up their vessels!

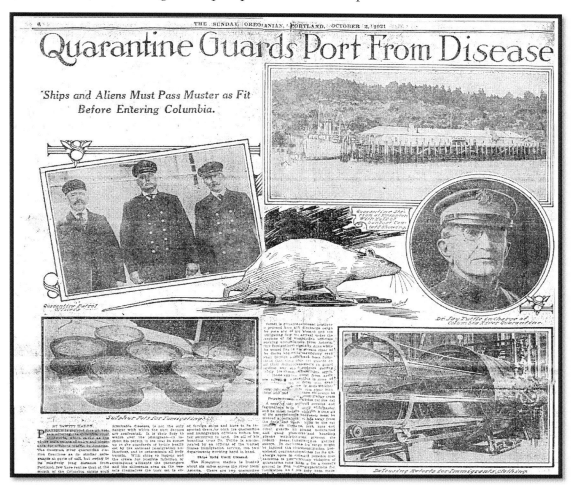

Ships from around the world were coming to the lower Columbia. The year the station opened ships arrived from Germany, Norway, Britain, Japan, Russia, France and Peru. 97 sailing vessels and 35 steam vessels were inspected, and a total of 6,120 people went through health inspection that year at the Knappton facility. The 1921 Oregonian article stated: "The recent enormous increase in offshore traffic for the Columbia river has served to accentuate the value of the services rendered by this station, until now it is taking rank among the first ten in the United States."

The same article went on to state: "Two decades of activity have made the Columbia river quarantine into a smooth working machine far superior to that in operation on Puget sound, and to date even more efficient. The importance of this work cannot be over-estimated." It ends on a decidedly patriotic note, "Uncle Sam has a big investment in the Columbia river quarantine station which is justified in its ability to make certain that incoming aliens are clean and fit to mingle with healthy humans and that danger of transferring disease from foreign countries is eliminated. During the last two years the crews at the quarantine station have had few idle spells, all this time there being a steady flow of oncoming and outgoing traffic. The government is ever on the watch and shipping men have been educated to realize the advantage of extreme vigilance where the health of the nation is concerned."

Immigrant Passengers Arriving by Ship in Columbia River c. 1900

Photo Courtesy of Columbia River Maritime Museum

In the 1880's many Europeans were immigrating to America in search of a better life. U.S. railroad and steamship companies traveled throughout Europe advertising the boundless opportunities that awaited those who came. Many young, single Norwegians came from the area north of the Arctic Circle where they eked out a meager living fishing for cod and doing some farming on the side. Some came through Ellis Island and came west by train. Among the other ports of entry listed in the naturalization papers were Astoria and Portland, Oregon, Port Huron and Sault Ste Marie in Michigan, San Francisco, California and Sumas,

48 Star Flag from the Station

Washington. Hagbart Johnsen paid $93.00 from his trip from Kjerringoy, Norway to Portland, Oregon in 1909. He settled in SW Washington on the Willapa River.

A long term and faithful employee at the Station was Ole Estoos, who emigrated from Norway when he was 18. He had been apprenticed as a teenager to a carpenter in Norway. It was his carpentry skills that brought him to Knappton when the government began the construction of the Quarantine Station. Original correspondence and purchasing forms written by Ole were left at the Station when it closed and have been preserved and are on display

Ole Estoos wore many hats through the years.

Photo Courtesy of Columbia River Maritime Museum

in the museum. Some of the supplies ordered were "Grandpa's Tar Soap," "Gold Dust" washing powder, and "Celluloid" starch. Ole retired in 1932.

Desk Made & Used by Ole Estoos at the Station

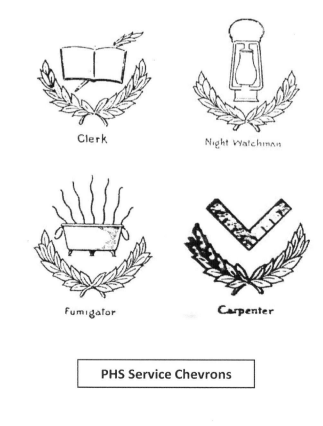

PHS Service Chevrons

53

UNITED STATES PUBLIC HEALTH AND MARINE-HOSPITAL SERVICE.

OFFICE OF MEDICAL OFFICER IN COMMAND,

COLUMBIA RIVER QUARANTINE STATION. *December 30th 1912,*

~~ASTORIA, OREG.~~

Medical Officer in Command U.S.P.H.S.
Columbia River Quarantine Station
                          Astoria, Oregon

   Sir:— I have the honor to make requisition for the following Article

4, renewals, B.S. & C. Edison primary battery
No. 5. And 8, being complete,

     Gasoline
     4in Manila rope
1, Grind stone fixtures
2, Small varnish brushes
2, 6in flat files
4, 10in flat files
6, Assorted files (pointed)
5, Iron blank nuts for ¾in. bolts

              Respectfully
              C. H. Estes
              Supervising Attendant

Supt of Laundry

Boatswain

Prescription Clerk

Yardman

Pilot

Public Health Service Uniform Chevrons from 1923 Manual
Pertaining to Quarantine Stations

Jens Hanson, "A Good Man"
Note the Official 'Orderly'
Chevron on his sleeve. c. 1909

Ole was one of many Scandinavians who worked at the Station. Others listed in the Station log include Louis Erickson, Nels N. Williamson, John Johnson, Hilbert Hanson, John Olsen, Jens Lervick. In a few instances, there are interesting comments in the log. A crewman on the *ELECTRO*, Mathue Johnson's performance was described "services perfunctory and indifferent." The log states that John Maack, a fireman on the *ELECTRO* was "A well-meaning, but very stupid and unreliable man," and Frank Williams performance rating states "Service ordinary. Given to over-indulgence in alcohol." Jens Hanson, who worked at the Station in about 1909 and whose descendants still reside in SW Washington was described as "A good man." Thaddeus Trullinger and his wife Georgia both were employed at the Station. Georgia worked as a cook.

Orderly

After Dr. Baylis Earle left the Station in 1906, Passed Assistant Surgeon John Milton Holt was assigned to duty there. Dr. Holt often traveled to represent the Service at regional medical meetings, according to the log. He also liked to vacation in Gearhart Park in Oregon. In 1911 Assistant Surgeon Jay Tuttle assumed command. Dr. Tuttle retired when he was 81, apparently in good health, but contracted pneumonia and died before he turned 82. He was often assisted by Dr. Pilkington of Astoria. In 1905 the Surgeon General of the United States, Walter Wyman, visited and inspected the Station.

Dr. Jay Tuttle

In the 1920's methods of inspection, fumigation and inoculation changed, and health practices were improving. In 1928 the Quarantine Office was relocated in Portland. Quarantine inspectors were no longer stationed at Astoria, but would come when necessary from Portland. Oscar Berg was one of those inspectors who came often. There was still a part time U.S. Quarantine doctor in

Astoria, Dr. Pilkington, and an assistant boarding officer, Dr. Hyde. Pilkington's administrative assistant was Anne Washer who served the PHS in Astoria for 24 years. In 1929, the use of cyanide gas replaced the sulfur pots. New disinfecting agents made it possible for ships to be cleaned at anchor nearer the Port of Astoria. Only extreme isolation cases were sent to Knappton Cove. And foreign immigration was curtailed. In 1907, the Japanese were excluded, and in 1924 a quota system for European nationalities went into effect. The Columbia River Quarantine Station was phased out and closed in 1938. The *Concord* was scrapped in Astoria. The handsome brass and glass starlite & ventilator was salvaged and is now on permanent display at the Columbia River Maritime Museum, and the beautiful carved wooden gangway entrance is housed in their archives. Airports were becoming the new 'ports of entry.' The only thing in use at the Station was a navigational aid on the dock maintained by the Bureau of Lighthouses. In 1949 the property was declared surplus, and it was put up for auction in 1950.

Ship *Agnes Oswald* at Station – 1903

Photo Courtesy of Columbia River Maritime Museum

NOVEMBER 16, 1899.

Messrs. GOODALL, PERKINS & CO.,
San Francisco, Cal.

Sir: Referring to your letter of the 8th instant, with regard to the inspection of your vessels plying between Victoria, British Columbia, and San Francisco after the hour of 6 p. m., I have to inform you that the matter has been taken under advisement, and that every endeavor will be made to arrange matters in such a way as to comply with all necessary sanitary precautions and at the same time give the least possible cause for complaint to commerce.

Respectfully,

WALTER WYMAN,
Surgeon-General, M. H. S.

JANUARY 9, 1900.

MEDICAL OFFICER IN COMMAND,
San Francisco Quarantine, Angel Island, Cal.

Sir: Referring to recent correspondence between Messrs. Goodall, Perkins & Co. and yourself with regard to the inspection of vessels from Canadian ports arriving at San Francisco after night, I have to inform you that where such vessels are provided with electric lights to facilitate the inspection you are authorized to do this inspection up to 10 o'clock at night in summer and 9 o'clock during winter months.

Respectfully,

WALTER WYMAN,
Surgeon-General, M. H. S.

COLUMBIA RIVER QUARANTINE; POST-OFFICE ADDRESS, VIA ASTORIA, OREG.

[Report of the medical officer in command, Asst. Surg. HILL HASTINGS. Assumed command under official orders of April 28, 1899.]

Columbia River Quarantine Station,
Astoria, Oreg., August 16, 1900.

Sir: I have the honor to report the transactions at this station during the fiscal year ended June 30, 1900, as follows:

QUARANTINE WORK.

Number of vessels inspected and passed	10
Number of vessels held for disinfection	28
Total	132

Treatment of vessels held for disinfection:

Hold disinfected	19
Forecastle and crews' effects disinfected	5
Cabin and staterooms disinfected	2
Baggage disinfected (number of pieces)	1,526

Causes for detention of vessels in quarantine:

(1) Plague epidemic at port of departure	16
(2) Yellow fever en voyage	1
(3) Beriberi en voyage	3
(4) Oriental immigrants aboard whose baggage required disinfection	8

Of the vessels whose holds were disinfected, 10 came from Honolulu, where plague was epidemic, necessitating fumigation to destroy rats. As there was no sulphur furnace provided, sulphur was burned in pots or on the ballast, and the hatches battened down for forty-eight hours. This effectually destroyed the rats, which were usually found dead in the open, where they had dropped after being smoked out of crevices and holes. Panama was responsible for the infection with yellow fever of four ships while in that port, causing 40 cases and 15 deaths. The infection, apparently, must have occurred while the vessels were discharging coal at one of the four little island coaling stations, about 3 miles from the city, and was the subject of a previous report.

Beriberi occurred on three vessels from the Orient—one from Manila, 8 cases and 1 death; one from Shanghai, 2 cases; and one from Kobe, 3 cases and 1 death. It

is worthy of note, in view of the question as to the cause of beriberi, that the first case of beriberi broke out on the Kobe vessel 8 weeks before entering that port and 153 days out from Philadelphia, and that the first case occurred on the Shanghai vessel 30 days before entering that port and 130 days out from New York. Nothing could be learned to explain the long incubation period of the disease. Neither vessel had touched at an intermediate port nor had changed food or water. In each case the captain was one of those afflicted. From the long voyage the men had become somewhat debilitated, but had not given any signs of scurvy or digestive troubles.

Number of persons inspected and passed quarantine:

Crew	3,899
European passengers	1,175
Oriental immigrants	1,046
Total	6,120

Number of persons detained in quarantine:

	97
	35
Total	132

On account of plague at San Francisco two Chinese from that port were held twelve days to complete incubation period.

Character of vessels inspected:

Sailing vessels	97
Steam vessels	35
Total	132

Nationality:

American	22
German	18
Norwegian	1
British	85
Japanese	1
Russian	1
French	3
Peruvian	1
Total	132

The degree of cleanliness and of good sanitary condition is represented in the order of the above classification. Of the most common vessels, American, German, and British, the latter presented the dirtiest and most ill-kept forecastles. The German sailors were apparently the best fed.

By order of the Bureau, July 1, 1899, medical inspection of alien immigrants was made at this station instead of at Portland, Oreg.

There were inspected and passed (chiefly Japanese)	552
Rejected	None.

Cost of maintenance of station:

Compensation of officers and employees	$4,824.70
Expenses of quarantine boarding steamer, including rent of same	2,225.34
Disinfectants	389.17
Incidentals	417.82
Total	7,857.03

CONSTRUCTION OF THE STATION.

The disinfection work during this fiscal year was done aboard ship with the use of emergency apparatus kept on the quarantine steamer Electric. This is a small tugboat that had been housed in for the accommodation of freight and passengers. The boat was leased in for the year at $150 per month, and, with a few changes, proved to be a very serviceable quarantine boat. The crew, consisting of captain, engineer, and deck hand, was regularly appointed in the service and assisted in the disinfecting work. At Astoria dock privileges were rented at $5 per month, and office room, heat, and lights for $10 per month.

In August the Department of Justice, through the office of United States Attorney Wilson R. Gay, Seattle, Wash., took up the matter of purchase of the Knappton Cannery property directly across the river from Astoria, which had been selected in October, 1898, as available for a quarantine station site. The price agreed on and approved by the Department at that time was $3,000.

The transfer of this property was effected on February 8, 1900, by the payment of this sum to the owners, the Eureka and Epicure Packing Company. Preliminary

New Dock at Station Viewed from River Beach

Photo Courtesy of Columbia River Maritime Museum

New Dock 1902

Photo Courtesy of Pacific County Historical Society

East End of Dock: Note the firewood stacked in building '7' used for heating shower water for immigrants going through inspection in dock '6' building.

Photo Courtesy of Pacific County Historical Society

Main Dock Building, same as the one marked '6' in picture above.

Note the *Electro* Moored at the East End of Dock

U.S.S. Concord moored at Station to house immigrants & crew who passed health inspection while their ship was fumigated. It took about 48 hours to disinfect a ship.

"Jimmie" from Ship *Roxburg*
with Two Monkeys

1994.29.116

Crew of *Roxburg*
Disinfecting Ballast on
Scow--1902

Photos Courtesy of
Columbia River
Maritime Museum

1994.29.111

4-Masted Square Rigged Ship at Station

Photos Courtesy of Columbia River Maritime Museum

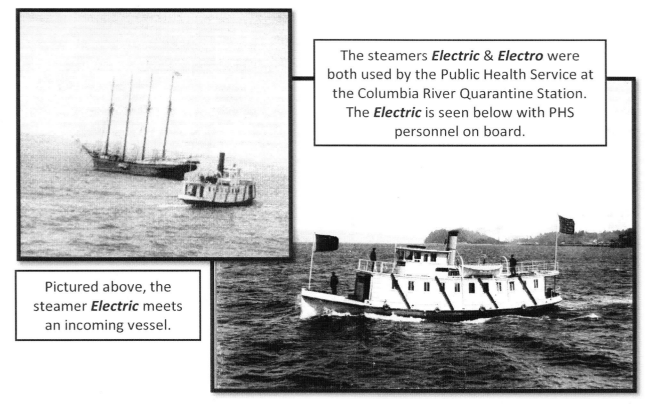

The steamers *Electric* & *Electro* were both used by the Public Health Service at the Columbia River Quarantine Station. The *Electric* is seen below with PHS personnel on board.

Pictured above, the steamer *Electric* meets an incoming vessel.

Clinical Photos from Patient at Station – 1903

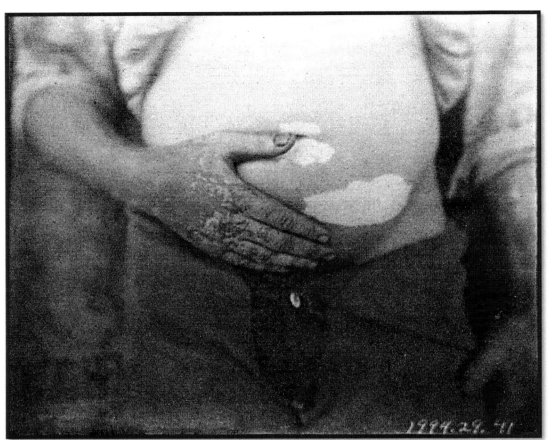

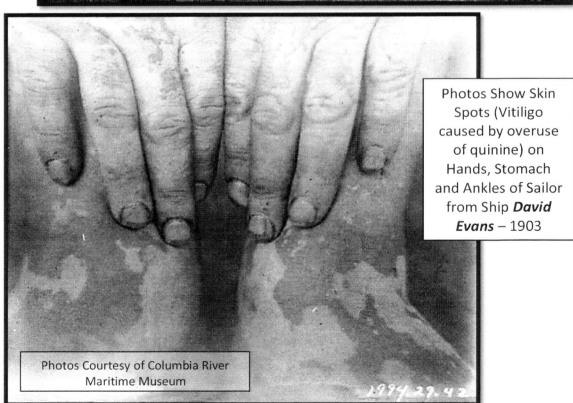

Photos Show Skin Spots (Vitiligo caused by overuse of quinine) on Hands, Stomach and Ankles of Sailor from Ship *David Evans* – 1903

Photos Courtesy of Columbia River Maritime Museum

Men Recovering from Small Pox

Thanks to Liisa Penner for finding this photo at the Clatsop County Heritage Museum

THE EARLY 1900's BROUGHT THOUSANDS OF IMMIGRANTS TO THE WEST COAST PORTS OF ENTRY

Photo Courtesy of Dept. of Health & Human Services, Program Support Center

Although Ellis Island handled the largest numbers of immigrants, there were other U.S. Ports of Entry. Angel Island, in San Francisco Bay, was among the other major west coast Ports of Entry. Here Asian immigrants arrive at Angel Island, men follow behind ladies, 1931.

We estimate about 100,000 immigrants passed through health inspection at Knappton Cove where the Quarantine Station was equipped for fumigating ships, bathing and inspecting immigrants & crews, and cleansing their clothing & baggage. Immigrants were then sent upriver to Portland to be processed for naturalization.

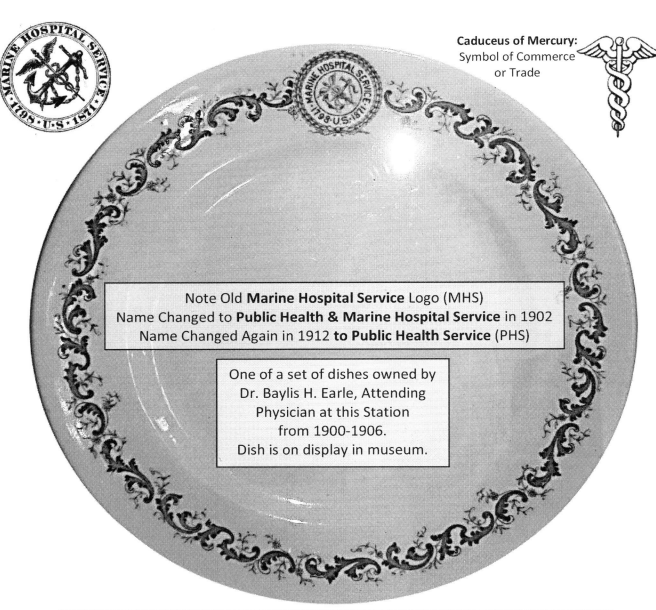

Caduceus of Mercury:
Symbol of Commerce
or Trade

Note Old **Marine Hospital Service** Logo (MHS)
Name Changed to **Public Health & Marine Hospital Service** in 1902
Name Changed Again in 1912 **to Public Health Service** (PHS)

One of a set of dishes owned by
Dr. Baylis H. Earle, Attending
Physician at this Station
from 1900-1906.
Dish is on display in museum.

Ceramic shard found in the Knappton Cove tidelands by Tom Bell, 2006. Note the USMHS marking which dates the piece to pre-1902.

From 1912 Public Health Bulletin Found on Site

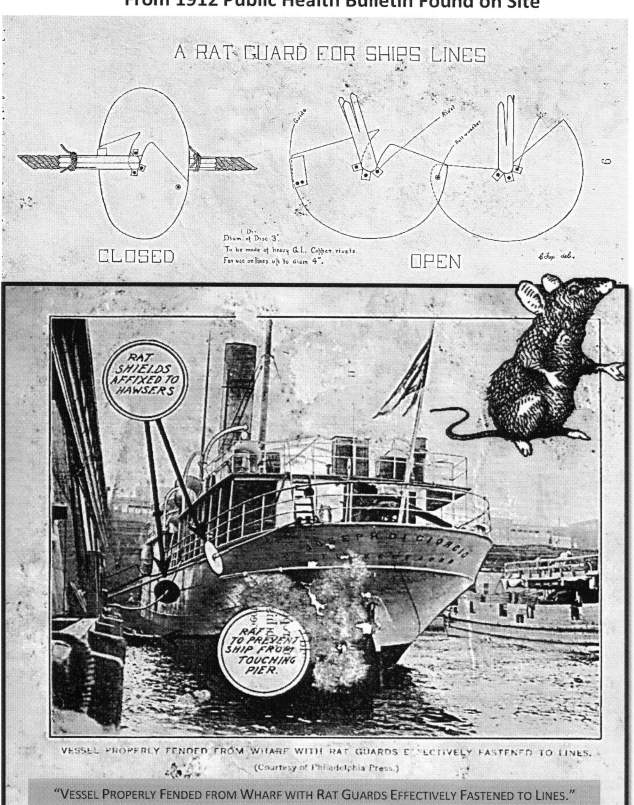

"VESSEL PROPERLY FENDED FROM WHARF WITH RAT GUARDS EFFECTIVELY FASTENED TO LINES."

SUPERFICIAL PALMAR ARCH.

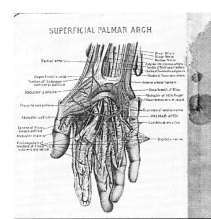

OCCIDENTAL MEDICAL TIMES

COMBINING THE

"Pacific Record of Medicine and Surgery" and the "Occidental Medical Times."

EDITED BY

JAMES H. PARKINSON, Sacramento.

LOUIS A.

Excerpts from Vintage
Medical Publications
found on Site

s, Sacramento.	THOS. W
n Francisco.	ALBERT
an Francisco.	A. W. 1
Y, San Francisco.	LEO NE
n Francisco.	PHILIP
y, San Francisco.	C. R. C
tt, San Francisco.	A. B. M

San Francisco, April, 1901.   NO. 4.
Single Copies, 20 Cents

MARCHAND'S EYE BALSAM

Therapeutic Philosophy.

"According to the fair play of the world let me have audience."

It will not hurt the most Scientific Doctor to take a glance at this.

The Antikamnia Chemical Co., St. Louis, Mo., U. S. A.

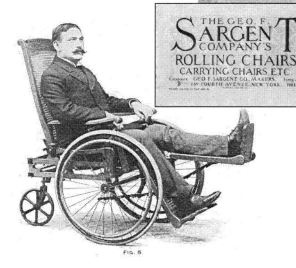

FIG. 5

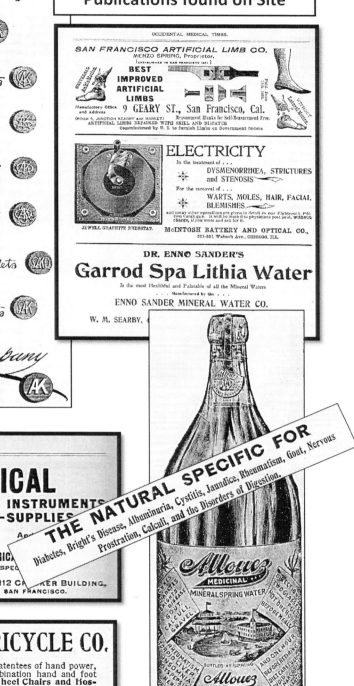
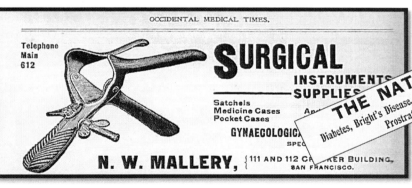
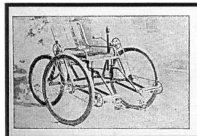
67

· U · S · QUARANTINE · STATION ·

COLUMBIA RIVER OREGON

Attendants' Quarters

ATTENDANTS' QUARTERS

Hospital

HOSPITAL

Carpenter Shop & Pumphouse

CARPENTER SHOP & PUMPHOUSE

Stable

STABLE

New Storage Tank

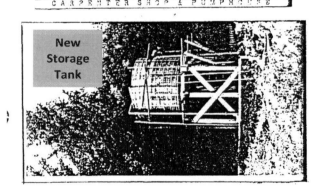

NEW STORAGE TANK

New Tank House

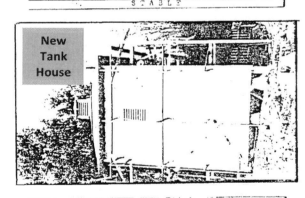

NEW TANK HOUSE

Wood & Supply House

WOOD & SUPPLY HOUSE

Old Blacksmith Shop

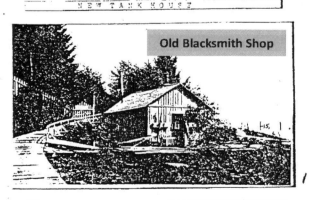

OLD BLACKSMITH SHOP

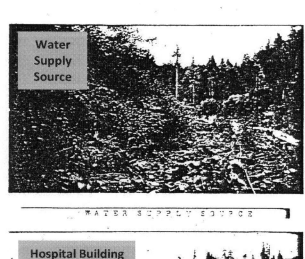

Water Supply Source

WATER SUPPLY SOURCE

Land Containing Water Supply

LAND CONTAINING WATER SUPPLY

Hospital Building

HOSPITAL BUILDING

Reservoir & Hose Reel House

RESERVOIR & HOSE REEL HOUSE

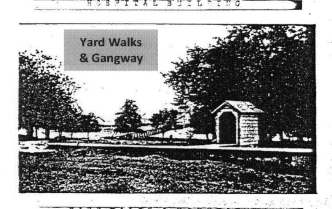

Yard Walks & Gangway

YARD WALKS & GANGWAY

Gangway to Wharf

GANGWAY TO WHARF

Gangway to Land

GANGWAY TO LAND

Wharf Construction Float

WHARF CONSTRUCTION FLOAT

69

COLUMBIA RIVER OREGON

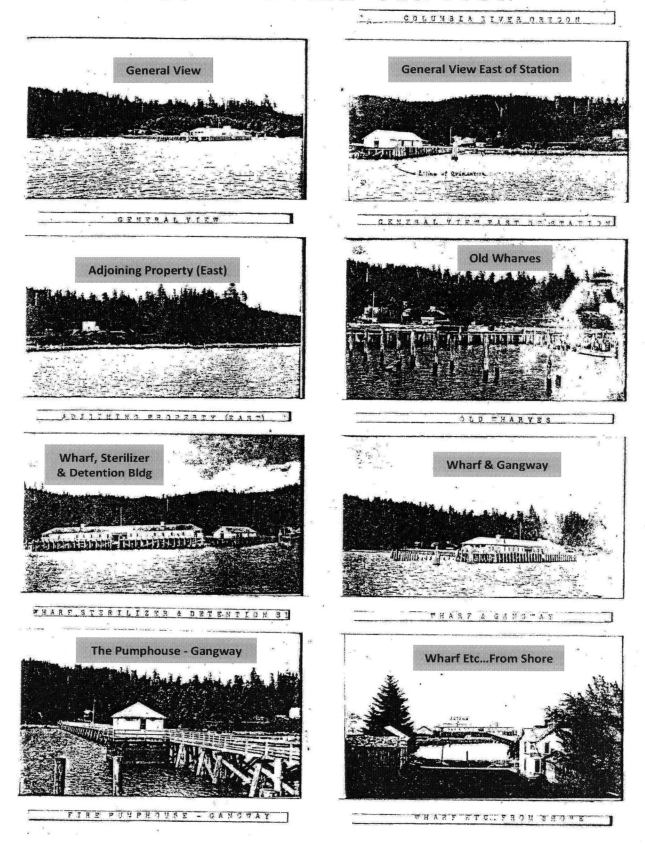

General View

GENERAL VIEW

General View East of Station

GENERAL VIEW EAST OF STATION

Adjoining Property (East)

ADJOINING PROPERTY (EAST)

Old Wharves

OLD WHARVES

Wharf, Sterilizer & Detention Bldg

WHARF, STERILIZER & DETENTION B?

Wharf & Gangway

WHARF & GANGWAY

The Pumphouse - Gangway

FIRE PUMPHOUSE - GANGWAY

Wharf Etc...From Shore

WHARF ETC...FROM SHORE

THE BEARMAN BUNGALOW

Adjoining the west section of the Quarantine Station is a piece of land upon which a small home was built in about 1935. Charles Bearman was hired on as General Mechanic in 1934. According to the Station log, Bearman was a somewhat assertive employee. He disregarded the ruling that no families of employees could live on the station grounds and immediately moved his family into the Superintendent's house. When the government found out, he was ordered to relocate his family. So Bearman built a home next to the Station – RIGHT next to the station. As a matter of fact, he built the house RIGHT ON the property line. The front door opened right onto the grounds. Now I have a strong suspicion that perhaps the Bearman children may have played on the Station property.

When the Station closed Bearman was separated from the USPHS and transferred to the Bureau of U.S. Lighthouses, and he moved his family across the river to Oregon. Eventually, he sold his house to a young newly married Finnish fisherman, Charley Mattson and his wife Cora. It wasn't until after the sale that Charley discovered that Bearman didn't even own the land on which the house sat! It belonged to the Hagerup family whose home was west of the Station. Seems Bearman had just a loose verbal agreement from Werner Hagerup to build his house there. Well, the Mattsons ended up buying just the land that the house sat on from Hagerup. But this time the Station had closed so Charley proceeded to enclose a nice little yard – all of which, naturally, jutted out onto the station grounds! So much for property lines. Charley also opted to raise chickens in the west end of the old abandoned Quarantine Hospital. And both Charley and the Hagerups moored their gillnetters and racked their nets at the old Quarantine dock. Pretty convenient.

And so it was kind of a shock to the locals when the government decided to auction off the old Station. But Dad quickly befriended them all and had no objections to the gillnet boats remaining at the dock providing the fishermen would help with maintaining the dock. All went well until Dad drew up a legal document allowing the Mattsons to keep their 'fenced in' yard as long as they resided there. He thought he was doing the Mattsons a favor but Charley was furious! We could never figure out why. He and Cora had no children so there were no direct heirs. Anyway, that began an ongoing feud between him and Dad that lasted their lifetimes. Soon after Cora died, Charley had health problems and went to live in a 'rest home.' And true to Dad's word, he had Charley's fence removed and a new chain link fence installed along the REAL property line. Of course, the new fence was installed RIGHT AGAINST the east wall and front door of Charley's house!

Charley managed to outlive Dad, but Dad had gotten his revenge. When Charley died, his house was sold and that place continued to be a thorn in our side. Since raw sewage could no longer be dumped into the creeks that emptied into the Columbia, septic tanks had to be installed. Since Charley's house had been vacant for a long period of time, a septic tank had never been put in. The new owners found out there was no room for a drain field since the house was built on that narrow strip of land between the Station and a creek. The only solution for them was a very expensive and complicated installation unless they could obtain easements and land purchases from us. And we didn't want to further subdivide our part of the Station. In fact, we'd been told that no further subdivision could occur. So the Bearman Bungalow was once again put on the market. Several deals fell through because of all the complications with the septic arrangements, and the owners contacted us to see if we would be interested in purchasing the old house.

We decided to put an end to the bickering and confusion and make the purchase ourselves. We felt it would, in the long haul, enhance our portion of the old Station. We deeded it over to our daughter and son-in-law with 'love and affection.' (Honestly, that's the legal phrase you use!) Charley and Clarence would be amazed. A state-of-the-art septic system has now been installed (1999), a new roof put on and the foundation repaired. With new wiring and lots of work, the little Bearman Bungalow once again provides shelter as a family vacation cottage.

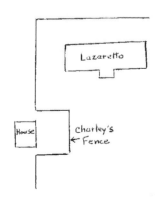

Home of Charles & Matilda Bearman

THE WOMEN OF KNAPPTON COVE

Much of history is just that – HIS STORY. So I'd like to take a closer look at the women of Knappton Cove and attempt to view the story from a feminine perspective. Admittedly, the women who have lived or camped at Knappton Cove from the early Chinooks to the present day owe their presence there to the men in their lives.

We already know that the Chinook women were adept at handling canoes and food preparation. Even in a male dominated society, the Chinook women could own property and take part in the village council. And they sure weren't worried about making a fashion statement – they wore very little! And remember they were described as ' good-natured' so evidently they were a pleasant lot, despite the hardships they must have endured. Their culture certainly did not embrace the 'Victorian moral code and double standard' of European and American tradition. When a husband died, 'ownership' of his wife was passed on to his brother. We do know that venereal disease became a health problem that plagued the Chinooks, as well as those early explorers.

Those Chinook gals must have been interested in Sacagawea, a Shoshone Indian, when she showed up with Lewis & Clark and all those other guys. And 'Janey,' as Clark called her, was also concerned with food preparation. Clark recorded that she was in favor of a place for wintering over where there were 'plenty of Potas' (roots). There are many interesting accounts written about Sacagawea – some accurate and some speculative, but all fascinating.

And then came Jane Barnes. She really did make a fashion statement and must have been a welcome curiosity for those Chinook women. Remember – her man drowned and then she was invited, but declined, to become a Chinook wife – one of several, no less. And I guess one might speculate that Jane was a pretty independent sort and most likely did not let any one man dominate her life.

So often, women are introduced into history by their connections to men. Sarah Frances Wilson, the wife of Job Lamley who established the Donation Land Claim at Knappton Cove was described as "the third cousin of President Woodrow Wilson, and descended from an ancestral line of William Penn, James Wilson and the Pegg family of Philadelphia, Pennsylvania." Never mind that she produced 9 children and ran a stately home on the banks of the Columbia River. And she must have befriended the newly wed Caroline Benjamin Knapp. The

Knapp's home was built "near the Lamley house." Caroline came in handy when she was granted power of attorney in 1871 to sign (maneuver?) some papers indicating that J.B. was having financial difficulties.

The cannery era at Knappton Cove makes absolutely no mention of any women at all. It is interesting to note that in later years, women took over many of the menial cannery jobs that the Chinese men did in earlier years. Of course, ships arrived with regularity, and ships were always spoken of in the feminine gender, as in "Ahoy, Matey, thar *she* sails." Legend has it that a Captain's vessel was as important to him as a wife and so was lovingly referred to as a lady, whose behavior incidentally could be either naughty or nice. Naturally, derogatory feminine terms were also frequently heard aboard ship when things malfunctioned.

When the Quarantine Station opened, as previously pointed out, no employee's wives or children were allowed on the premises. Of course, we know that 'rule' didn't always hold because of the wonderful summer picnic pictures taken on the grounds in the early 1900's. On that particular day there were **LOTS** of women. There were also separate bathrooms out on the dock for women arriving on ships. And we know that the women and girls of the Hagerup family had

Picnic on Station Grounds, Front Porch of Cannery Superintendent's House—Whose New Use was Housing Station Personnel, early 1900's.

Photo Courtesy of Columbia River Maritime Museum

passes which allowed them to enter the station grounds. Their government passcard was the size of a postcard and signed by the President of the United States. And according to the Station log Georgia Trullinger, whose husband was a PHS employee at the Station, was hired on as a cook for a short time.

The Station log also notes several women employees who must have either worked there or at least visited often. Two women employees appear in that early photo of Public Health Service employees, Mrs. Annie Abraham and Madge Sovey. Madge was detailed as a clerk and, once again, the important male connection shows up! When she submitted her resignation on January 31, 1906 the log states that she was leaving to "marry Mr. Willard Rush of Kansas City – a lineal descendant of the celebrated Dr. Benjamin Rush." Remember that Dr. Rush was the noted doctor who instructed Meriwether Lewis before he left on the Lewis & Clark Expedition. It is also of note and significant that she was replaced by Miss Mary Fossett from Maine at a salary of $50/month – the same as for men clerks. It is a credit to the Public Health Service that policy dictated equal pay for any grade job held – man or woman. The log also notes that her salary was increased to $60/month in March of 1907— good pay for anyone at that time.

Annie

Madge

Men & Women Enjoying a Picnic on Station Grounds, Early 1900's

Ole Estoos

Photo Courtesy of Columbia River Maritime Museum

Ole Estoos was a bachelor when he first worked at the Station but subsequently married an attractive schoolteacher, a widow with three children who taught school at Knappton. His preserved correspondence shows many 'corrections' added by his wife. Nora Bollinger Lynch was born in Kansas and came west with her family when she was a youngster. The newly married Estoos couple lived adjacent to the Station. They produced two sons, Norman and Darrell (Dale). Nora let each of her two older daughters (by her first marriage) pick a name for the youngest baby and they chose Darrell and Andrew. She herself chose the name Loren. He shortened that long name to Dale

– the first letters of all of his given names. When Ole retired in 1934, they moved across the river to Oregon where some of their descendants still reside. Their deserted home at Knappton burned in 1936.

And don't forget Matilda Bearman who must have been a resilient soul. Surely those Bearman children played on the Station grounds.

Clara Hagerup continued to live west of the Station after her husband Werner died. The Hagerups had built their first home there in 1907. That house

Clara

burned and they rebuilt in 1912. Werner was a fisherman in the summer and worked at the Knappton Mill during the winter. Clara's oldest son Harold lived with her. Her other 4 children were frequent visitors, including William pictured here when serving in the U.S. Navy. Her daughters, Edna and Inez both inherited their mother's fun-loving spirit. Clara lived to a ripe old age and baked bread almost every day of her life. And by the 1940's, Cora Mattson, Charley's wife was a

William Hagerup

neighbor. Cora was a shy, friendly, simple woman and not well educated, but had a flourishing, beautiful yard and garden. Flowers from both women's gardens remain today. They both gave my mother lots of 'starts,' as well. Two other Scandinavian fishermen's wives lived nearby. Irene Gunderson and her husband Art had a lovely home, which still stands. Irene was an immaculate housekeeper and made tasty cookies that were always at the ready when Clara and Larry and I visited her. Grace Seablom and her husband Gus were the other neighbors. None of these three ladies had children but Grace was a colorful character who sometimes looked like a phantom wafting by in her long, flowing skirts. In 1927 Grace had come here from San Francisco and married Gus, a Swedish-speaking Finn who had emigrated from Finland. She wrote to friends describing her marriage "...joined in marriage...for life, we two: who were born a whole wide world apart and spoke in different tongues – We are together – No matter what comes..." She was indeed a poet. Here's a poem she wrote about Knappton.

"Rhymes of the Place of Memories"
Knappton, Washington
by Grace Seablom

WOODLAND HOME

They said, you have gone to the jungles – when I left the city
    for a home 'neath the trees.
But – how could they – the restless ones – understand the peace—
    that comes like a mother's caress, to tell a tired heart to rest?
The dawn – with its glorious color – bird's songs and
    the sweet scented breeze –
Noontime and the welcome extended 'neath shady trees,
Twilight and each drowsy flower – nods its sleepy head –
While frogs in the woodland chant, go-to-bed, go-to-bed.
Night – and the moon in its splendor – produces its path of dreams
    on the breast of my well-loved river –
        Columbia, Majestic, Serene.

And that brings us to my mother, Katharine – introducing another element into the Knappton Cove story. Since our family came from Portland, we were pretty much considered 'outsiders' and 'city' people. But when Dad retired and they sold their home in Portland, they became full-time residents also. Mother was always a history buff, and she collected and saved many of the artifacts (as did my brother Tom) that remained at the Station. She also liked to garden and could often be seen driving off the pesky deer when they were nibbling on her roses. But one thing she didn't like was, of all things, boats. She had a fear of the water and as she had never learned to swim had a real aversion to boating. But she loved fish and seafood. When she did get into a boat, it was with reluctance. When Dad, at retirement, purchased his pride and joy, a 24-foot

The "Puker"

aluminum **STARCRAFT**, she dubbed it *"The Puker."* Need I say more?

And the ladies who came to fish and camp with their husbands added

Bernita Zimmerman with a 'Big One'

another dimension to the scene. Bernita Zimmerman and her husband Orville, long-time friends of my folks spent a great deal of time there. Ellen Magette, a truly dedicated sports fisherwoman, camped there every summer with her husband Bob. My brother Tom and sister-in-law Georgia spent many a summer at Knappton with their kids – Noreen, Morgan and Susan. They trekked northward from California for years since Tom, a teacher, had summers off. Occasionally my brother Bob and his

Mom in Office Selling Herring Bait to Bernita

wife Charlotte visited with their girls, Laura and Linda. A newcomer to the scene came as a surprise when late in life Harold Hagerup married Verlie Peterson, as outspoken a woman as you'd ever meet! Verlie seemed to know it all, and you'd better not tell her otherwise.

And then, of course, there was me, and my family and grandkids. Our own kids, Heather and Paul spent plenty of time at their grandparent's. They, too, played endlessly on the river beach, went fishing, hiking in the woods, and spent numerous weekends and holidays at Knappton Cove. "Over the river and through the woods to grandmother's house we go..." was a familiar refrain as we traveled to their home. In later years, our grandkids, Katie and Madeline Henry and Mitchell and Tori Anderson came to play at Knappton Cove. Our daughter Heather Bell Henry, along with her husband Ken, has taken on the dubious honor of assisting me with the museum. Paul and his wife Carolyn also get involved frequently.

Heather & Paul on Knappton Beach

For several years after Dad died, my brother Bob and a new wife, Jenny lived in the folk's home. Tom and Georgia now own the middle portion of the property and have constructed a complementary building – workshop/garage/additional living quarters – alongside the old mess hall. Linda Bell Armstrong and her husband Marty purchased and are restoring the folk's old house. That house is the oldest building left on the property and thankfully, Marty has the necessary skills to take on that big project. And there is now another woman who resides at Knappton Cove. In 1995, Francesca and John Valentine acquired the shell of a Coast Guard building at Cape Disappointment,

Coast Guard Building

barged it upriver and had it placed on land they'd purchased on the hill directly behind the old station. After a beautiful restoration job, their home blends in perfectly with the old buildings of the Quarantine Station. Sadly, the old Hagerup house, in disrepair, was used as a practice burn by the Chinook Fire Department. The Hagerup family's attempts to get the old place back were unsuccessful.

Mention has to be made here of three young girls from Naselle High School who in 1998 researched and constructed a marvelous display "Triumph Over Disease" which they entered in the state's History Day Competition. Serene Stambaugh, Veronica Anderson and Clarissa Stewart won top honors in their category. Their award was a wonderful, handsome cement historical marker they designed which capsulizes the importance of the Columbia River Quarantine Station to the control of infectious disease at the mouth of the river. Their marker is proudly displayed in front of the old hospital building.

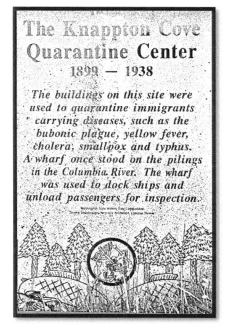

The Knappton Cove
Quarantine Center
1899 — 1938

The buildings on this site were used to quarantine immigrants carrying diseases, such as the bubonic plague, yellow fever, cholera, smallpox and typhus. A wharf once stood on the pilings in the Columbia River. The wharf was used to dock ships and unload passengers for inspection.

NHS students explore area's immigrant history

NASELLE—When they searched for a History Day project for teacher Dominic Urbano's Naselle High School history class, Serene Stambaugh, Veronica Anderson and Clarissa Stewart hadn't figured on studying flea fumigation and ship contamination.

They also didn't figure on being special guests and speakers at the Public Health Service's 200th anniversary celebration ceremony at the Knappton Cove Quarantine Center July 25.

Originally the trio had targeted the history of an old warship built in the Naselle area. A research lead took them to the Knappton Cove Quarantine Center where, impressed by the protective role the center played during heavy immigration to this country between 1899 and 1939, they immediately changed course. Their report on the center's history won local and regional competition awards, and at state level copped the Historical Marker Award.

The engraved granite historical marker, contains a message written by the students that reads: "The Knappton Cove Quarantine Center, 1899-1938. The buildings on this sight were used to quarantine immigrants carrying diseases such as the bubonic plague, yellow fever, cholera, smallpox and typhus.

"A wharf once stood on the pilings in the Columbia River. The wharf was used to dock ships and unload passengers for inspection." At the bottom of the plaque is an illustration by Stambaugh.

The quarantine center, presently owned by Nancy Bell, was one of four entry points on the West Coast processing immigrants. Some 132 ships and 6,120 people were inspected during its first year of operation.

The girls say the project was "surprisingly fun." They are looking forward to the Public Health Service ceremony where they will display their award-winning project. They hope—because the Lewis and Clark trail leads immediately past the center—that the plaque will help direct more visitors to the center.

The July 25 Public Health Service anniversary ceremony begins at 2 p.m. and includes a tour of the center. The center is regularly open Saturday afternoons during the summer. For more information, call (503) 738-5206.

STAN THOMPSON photo

Naselle High School students, above l-r, Serene Stambaugh, Veronica Anderson and Clarissa Stewart, were, through a high school history assignment, responsible for a 32- x 20-inch granite commemorative plaque being placed at the Knappton Cove Quarantine Center.

CHINOOK OBSERVER **FUN**

Tuesday, June 30, 1998

So you see, the influence of women at Knappton Cove is a significant part of the story. And because of my gender, I just wanted to make that clear. Indeed, if it weren't for the women in our family, the historical impact might be lost. Credit must be given at this point, however, to a MAN, Larry Weathers, who did the extensive research required to gain National Historic Registry designation. Of course, Larry must have an outstanding mother. But I have to admit we couldn't have done it if it weren't for my main man, Rex Anderson. After all, someone has to fix that weird old plumbing and replace worn-out parts of which there are so many. And for that we are truly grateful. A-MEN.

RECIPES FROM KNAPPTON COVE

So much of the history at our cove happened because of the savory salmon. And that brings us to eating. Here are recipes that I grew up with. Obviously, salmon was a mainstay in our family. From the first spring runs of Chinook up the Columbia into the Sandy River to the last of the canned salmon in late spring, salmon was a big part of my life. We ate salmon at least once a week all year long. We ate it fresh, canned, smoked, fried, baked or broiled. And I still love it. The easiest way to fix it is to just open a can and spread the salmon on soda crackers. Yum! Here are two other ways Mom prepared canned salmon.

CREAMED SALMON

1 6oz. can salmon (I also remove the skin and bones, but that's
optional)
1 T. butter
1 T. flour
¾ cup milk

Melt the butter in a saucepan. Add the flour and stir constantly for about 1 minute. Slowly add the milk, stirring constantly until the mixture thickens. Add the can of salmon along with the liquid, breaking the salmon apart with a fork. Season to taste with salt and pepper. Serve over buttered toast or biscuits. To jazz up this basic recipe, you can sauté chopped green onions, celery and/or mushrooms before adding the flour. Frozen peas can also be added along with the canned fish. Salt & pepper to taste.

SALMON LOAF

16 oz. can of salmon
2 eggs
1 ½ cups liquid (salmon juice plus milk)
3 cups coarse soda cracker crumbs.
2 T. lemon juice
2 tsp. minced onion
¼ tsp. each salt & pepper

Flake salmon, removing skin and bones if desired. Stir in eggs. Lightly fold in remaining ingredients. Pour into loaf pan or casserole dish. Bake for about 45" in a 350 degree oven. **NOTE:** This recipe is easy to cut in half by using the smaller cans of salmon. Mom always served this with her homemade tartar sauce.

81

MOM'S TARTAR SAUCE

Chopped Dill Pickles (Mom made her own – about ½ cup)
About ¼ cup mayonnaise
2 tsp. lemon or pickle juice
¼ tsp. horseradish (optional)

Stir all ingredients together. Don't worry about exact amounts – Mom never actually measured the ingredients, and neither do I. Sometimes I add a little fresh or dried dill and garnish with parsley.

MOM'S DILL PICKLES

Fresh scrubbed small pickling cucumbers
1 quart vinegar
2 quarts water
1 scant cup salt (about ¾ cup, I guess)
Fresh dill
Garlic cloves (peeled)

Pack cucumbers in sterilized canning jars with dill and garlic liberally mixed throughout. Put liquids and salt in pan and bring to boiling point. Pour over cucumbers in jars and seal. Makes about 5 quarts.

EASY WAYS TO FIX FRESH SALMON

1. Cut into 1" steaks. Melt some butter in a heavy pan and fry steaks, turning once or twice, until meat flakes easily.

2. Cut into 1" steaks and barbecue on grill or broil until fish flakes easily.

3. Cut into 1" steaks and poach in a little water with some white wine added until done.

4. Wrap cleaned small fish or roast-sized portions in heavy duty aluminum foil. Cook on outside barbecue or in oven until fish is cooked through – no longer transparent. Check often and be sure not to overcook. * Insert onion and/or lemon or orange slices in fish cavity before wrapping in foil, if desired.

Serve all of the above with Mom's Tartar Sauce! Garnish with lots of parsley and lemon slices or wedges.

The commercial fishermen at Knappton Cove often gave us fresh sturgeon because they weren't paid very much for it. That was back when hardly anybody knew about sturgeon, except the locals. It was a new taste for me, and I loved it. And it had a bonus as well – no bones to worry about. Sturgeon, an ancient lower invertebrate, has only cartilage along the top of its back. Now sturgeon has become a delicacy, very expensive and much sought after!

GRANDMA HAGERUP'S BOILED STURGEON

I remember my mother's surprise at how good this was. She'd never heard of just boiling fish, even though it was a common practice among the Scandinavians. All you do is place good-sized chunks of sturgeon meat into a pot of boiling water and as soon as it's no longer transparent, it's done. And I might add very tasty. Of course, we always ate it accompanied by Mom's Tartar Sauce. Sturgeon is also delicious as broiled or barbecued steaks or poached. Fix just as you would any other fish steak.

83

DAD'S SMOKED FISH

Dad had his own smoker and made lots of smoked salmon and sturgeon. Boy, was that good stuff! He always served plenty of it as an appetizer. Here's his recipe typewritten with his 'hunt & peck style' on his old Smith-Corona typewriter.

BRINE SOLUTION FOR SMOKING FISH & MEAT

To $\frac{1}{2}$ gal. of h2o; two cups of rock salt ; one cupof brown sugar;one teaspoon of black pepper; one teaspoon worchester sauce; small clove of garlic slivered; bay leaves and other spicesif desired.
Soak fish in brine for six hrs. remove and put thru two rinses of cold h2o; dry with paper towells and let stand until glaze formsabout six hrs

Smoke for 12hrs for canning; Longer if kept in refrigerator for snacks.
DO NOT DEEP FREZE SMOKED FISH

C. V. Bell at the helm of his boat – one of his favorite places.

CLAMS & OYSTERS

We often traveled to the Long Beach Peninsula to dig for razor clams. What an adventure that was. Dad carefully instructed me in the proper way to dig. Place the back of your clam shovel straight up and parallel with the ocean. Dig two quick shovelfuls, and then get down on your hands and knees and reach carefully into the hole, feeling for the clam. If you do it right, the clam will be on the shore side of the hole and you can gently scoop (or rather sort of pull) the clam out of the hole. If you get frantic and grab onto the clam in a hurry you can get a nasty cut – that's why they're called RAZOR clams. Or you might just end up pulling the neck off and the clam will 'get away.' Unfortunately, the digging just "isn't what it used to be," but I still get a thrill out of pulling a perfect clam out of a hole. And there is nothing more succulent than a fresh perfectly fried razor clam. Of course, cleaning the clams is quite a process and too hard to explain. You'll just have to have someone show you how to do that. If I'm available I'll be glad to demonstrate – I actually kind of like cleaning clams. My kids hate it. The folks had good friends, the Kemmerers, who frequently brought them fresh oysters – another succulent treat. Fix them the same way you prepare clams.

FRIED RAZOR CLAMS (ALSO OYSTERS)

First prepare 3 flat containers – fill one with cracker crumbs (either prepared or put soda crackers in a bag and use a rolling pin to crush the crackers into crumbs); fill another with flour and the third with 1 or 2 beaten eggs with just a little water added. Now, dip the clam (or oyster) FIRST in the flour, coating it thoroughly. The SECOND step is to dip it in the beaten eggs, again coating thoroughly. The LAST step is to roll it in the cracker crumbs and set it aside. Your fingers will get real gooey doing all this so be prepared to wash or wipe them off a few times during the process. The amounts of cracker crumbs, flour and eggs will depend upon how many clams you're preparing. So if you run out – just replenish them. (Whatever is left, you can roll into a ball, fry it and give it to the dog.) After the clams (oysters) are breaded, heat a little vegetable oil (enough to cover bottom of pan) in a heavy skillet. When oil sizzles, place clams (oysters) in pan. When coating is nice and brown, turn clams (oysters) over gently and brown on other side. It just takes a few minutes on each side – don't overcook or they'll be tough.

Now the trick to serving clams and oysters is to have everything else done and ready or already on the table! They are best eaten right out of the frying pan. *Now for some additional TIPS.* You can gently pound the clam necks to tenderize them a bit before you bread them and if the oysters are too big, just cut them in half and make little ones out of them. Nobody ever seems to notice this and they think you are serving those elegant small oysters.

Another clam readily available in the NW is the small 'littleneck' or sometimes called butter clam. These are small round cockle-shelled clams and also delicious. All you have to do is buy them at the grocery store or dig them up yourselves (much easier, but muddier, than the razor clams), wash them off thoroughly, and steam them in a little boiling water. You can add a little white wine to the water if you like. When they pop open, they're done. Serve them with melted butter with a little garlic added and lots of good bread to sop up the juices.

CLAM CHOWDER

I just can't stand to use good razor clams for chowder, but sometimes I cut off the necks for that. However, once in a while I break down and chop up perfectly good razor clams and make this chowder.

>2 large potatoes (or several smaller ones cut into bite-sized chunks)
>2 or 3 pieces of bacon (cut in small pieces)
>1/2 cup chopped celery
>2 green onions (chopped)
>2 or more cups milk
>Diced clams (1/2 cup or more)
>Chopped parsley & 2 T. butter

Fry bacon pieces and pour off most of the grease. Add celery and onions and sauté lightly. Add potatoes and cover with water. Bring to a boil and cook until potatoes are fork tender. Add milk and clams and heat through. Sprinkle with chopped parsley & butter and serve.

DUNGENESS CRAB

Well, it just doesn't get much better than gorging on fresh NW crabmeat. And pretty darn easy, besides. Naturally, the tastiest way is to catch them yourself and cook them right on the spot. Just plunge the fresh crabs into boiling water and when they turn orange, they're done. But they're also readily available in season at the grocery store or fish market – already cooked. Be sure to ask that the backs be removed, and you won't even have to clean them. Pull off the legs and cut the back into chunks. Crack the shells a bit with a nutcracker and serve the crab in a big bowl. Put nutcrackers on the table and nut-picks if you have them. If you don't, just use one the pointy claw ends for a pick. Spread the table with newspapers or oilcloth. With a 'newspaper tablecloth,' cleanup is easy – just wad the whole mess up when you're done and throw it in the trash. TIP: All that crab debris doesn't take long to become a smelly mess so if your garbage pick-up is several days away, bundle the remains in a big plastic garbage bag and store it in the freezer until garbage day arrives.

A real purist won't need anything to accompany good crab, but a little drawn butter with garlic can't be beat. Cracked crab is good served with soda crackers or French bread. Mom always had an alternate 'dip' because butter was 'too expensive.'

MOM'S DIP FOR CRAB

Mix about 1/2 cup of mayonnaise with a couple spoonfuls of catsup. Add a little bit of lemon juice, some salt and pepper and stir thoroughly. Surprisingly simple and good.

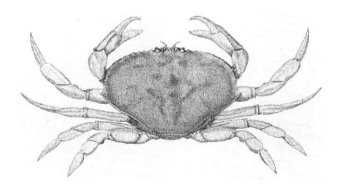

PAN FRIED TROUT

Once in awhile, Dad would take us trout fishing in nearby streams. Fried trout was always a real treat and still one of my favorites, even though you have to watch out for those pesky little bones. To prepare the cleaned fish, dip in flour seasoned with salt and pepper and then fry quickly in hot oil. When it's nice and crispy and cooked through, serve immediately. Nice with a little wedge of lemon on the side. So good! And remember the tom-cod that we caught with Harold Hagerup? They can be prepared just like fresh trout.

ACCOMPANIMENTS TO FISH & SEAFOOD

The abundance of fish and seafood here in the Pacific Northwest is something to treasure. It doesn't require much as an accompaniment. Any variety of vegetables – steamed asparagus, green string beans, corn-on-the-cob – all go well with seafood. Potatoes – boiled, mashed, fried or baked and a fresh salad or coleslaw round out the meal. Rice and pilaff are other good choices.

MEAT

Even though Dad was an avid fisherman, he was a 'meat, gravy and potatoes' man. But since he also liked to hunt, we always had plenty of venison, duck or pheasant. Mom fixed a mean pot roast (whether it be venison, elk or beef) – cooking it over a period of several hours in a slow oven until the meat just fell off the bones. She prepared game birds pretty much the same way – lots of cooking time in a slow oven. She always stuck an onion inside the bird's cavity to 'tame the wild flavor.' Of course, we also ate traditional meats – ham or turkey at holiday times and beef when we ran out of venison.

VEGETABLES & FRUIT AT THE COVE

The Lamley's (remember the donation land claim) had planted an orchard at Knappton Cove in the mid 1800's. Many of the old fruit trees still remain. We had lots of apples, some pears and cherries, and of course the wild blackberries and coast huckleberries, as well. Mom often made what she called good old-fashioned applesauce – sliced peeled apple pieces boiled in just enough water to cover with a little cinnamon and sugar added when apples were soft. She also made wonderful fruit pies.

MY MOM'S BASIC PIE CRUST

2 cups flour
1 cup shortening
1 tsp. baking powder
pinch of salt
less than 1/2 cup COLD water

Cut shortening into dry ingredients with a fork or pastry blender until mixture resembles the size of peas. Add the COLD water a little at a time, but do not over-mix. Handle as little as possible – just until it all sticks together fairly well. Roll out on floured board or pastry cloth to make crusts. This recipe makes enough for a top and bottom crust. Mother always baked the 'trimmings' from the pastry dough with a little sugar and cinnamon mixture on top – which we ate up immediately after they browned in the oven – SO GOOD.

FRUIT PIES & COBBLERS

For berry pies, mix about 1 cup sugar mixed with 1/2 cup flour with about 4 cups of berries. A bit of lemon juice (about 1 T) can be added to enhance the flavor. Put a little bit of flour and sugar into the bottom pie shell before adding the berry mixture – this helps absorb some of the juice. Add a few small chunks of butter. Fold top shell in fourths, cut a few slits and open up and place on top of berry mixture. Trim excess crust. For apple pie, add a T. of cinnamon. We also made lots of fruit cobblers – just following the directions on the Bisquick box. Mom made 'hard sauce' to go on the cobbler or served it with ice cream. To make the 'hard sauce' start with a lump of soft butter, add about a cup of powdered sugar, a little bit of vanilla and just enough milk to make a stiff mixture. Place a good-sized dollop on top of warm pie or cobbler and it will melt into the dessert. YUM.

Sometimes our relatives from California would bring us fresh lemons. And, of course, lemon just seems to compliment fish perfectly. We also often purchased farm fresh eggs from the 'Egg Lady' whose farm we passed just before we reached Knappton. All I can remember about her is that she always had eggs to sell and her young son would always dive under the kitchen table shouting "Air Raid." Here are two great recipes that Mom fixed using those fresh eggs and lemons.

LEMON MERINGUE PIE

One 9" pie shell
3 T. cornstarch
1 cup sugar
4 T. fresh lemon juice
1 T. butter
3 eggs (separated)

Combine cornstarch with sugar in top of double boiler. Add lemon, butter and 3 egg yolks (beaten). Mix well. Then add 1 1/2 cups boiling water very slowly. Cook over hot water until thick. Cool. Pour into pastry shell.

Meringue Topping: Beat egg whites until almost stiff. Then add 6 T. sugar. Beat until stiff. Arrange on top of pie to entirely cover filling. Bake in slow over (300 degrees) for about 30."

MOTHER'S CHESS PIES
One of her specialties

1 cup sugar
1/2 cup butter
a little nutmeg or vanilla
3 egg yolks (Save whites for meringue – prepare as above)
small pie shells (muffin tins work well)

Cream butter and sugar. Add egg yolks & flavoring. Place about 1/2 cup of mixture in small individual pie shells. Cook until slightly brown. Add meringue and set in oven to brown.

We made lots of berry jams – just following the directions on the Pectin package. Mother had her own secret berry patch for the little native blackberries. But she had a neat trick she used with the larger, introduced blackberries (Evergreen and Himalayas – which are seedier than the small native berries). She used a food mill to grind up about most of the washed berries and added them to the remaining 2 cups of the whole berries – this takes out a lot of the seeds.

In his retirement years, Dad planted a vegetable garden, which was pretty productive. He used crab shells for enriching the soil and it really worked. He did especially well with snow peas and green beans. He even had some limited success with artichokes. Fresh vegetables were always prepared simply – mostly just steamed until crisp tender and served with a little salt & pepper and a dollop of butter.

COOKIES & CANDY

YUMMY COOKIES (AND THEY ARE)

1/2 cup shortening or butter
1 cup sugar
2 eggs
1 tsp. vanilla
1 1/2 cup flour
1 tsp. baking powder
1/2 tsp. salt

Cream shortening and sugar. Add eggs one at a time. Beat 1 minute each. Add vanilla and dry ingredients. Pat into 8" square greased baking pan. Make a brown sugar meringue with 1 egg white (beaten until pretty stiff), 1 cup brown sugar and 1/2 cup chopped walnuts. Spread over top of cookie dough. Bake for 25" @ 375 degrees. Cut in squares.

PRESERVED GINGER COOKIES

This recipe is from an old Good Housekeeping magazine -- probably from the 30's or 40's. It's especially appropriate for boaters because candied ginger was traditionally used to prevent or control seasickness.

2 cups brown sugar
1 cup butter (This should be REAL butter.)
2 eggs

Cream the above ingredients together and then add:

3 cups flour
1 1/2 tsp. baking soda
1 1/2 tsp. baking powder
1/2 cup chopped preserved candied ginger

Shape into 2" rolls wrapping the dough in wax paper. Refrigerate. When thoroughly chilled, slice into thin pieces and place on greased cookie sheet. Bake in preheated 375 degree oven for 10-12" – until just nicely browned. My daughter and I like to serve these cookies at our Open Houses and Teas because they're delicious and this recipe makes a LOT.

MEXICAN CREAMS

This recipe – always a favorite – has been in our family for as long as I can remember. It most likely came from an old Good Housekeeping magazine, too.

        2 1/2 cups sugar
        1 cup milk
        1 cup chopped walnuts
        1 tsp. vanilla
        lump of butter
        Additional 1/2 cup sugar caramelized (In a small pan over a hot
burner stir constantly until the sugar melts and turns to a caramel colored liquid.
Be careful – this stuff is HOT!)

Boil sugar and milk in large pan. Add caramelized sugar. Continue to cook, stirring constantly, until it forms a soft ball when tested in a cup of cold water. (Drip a little bit off the end of the spoon that you're stirring with into the cold water.) Remove mixture from stove. Add vanilla and butter. Beat until creamy. Add nuts and pour into buttered pan. Cut into squares when cool. You just can't believe how good this candy is until you try it.

The incredible variety of good food we had to eat was truly amazing. It didn't hurt that Mom was a real good cook. She majored in Home Economics in college so she was always concerned about serving nutritionally balanced meals. Her family's motto was "moderation and variety in all phases of life." Pretty sensible. She lived over 98 years. Dad, who wasn't as cautious about his body, including football injuries and occasionally imbibing in a boilermaker and often enjoying a cold beer, only lived to be 87. Probably should have eaten more fish.

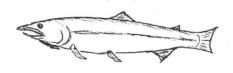

WHAT NOW?

At the beginning of this new millennium, I am hopeful that the story of Knappton Cove will provide a link between the past and the future – and that lessons learned through the past several centuries will help us make good choices for the future. The rich ethnic mix of humanity that set foot here throughout history is perhaps the most significant factor. Cultural diversity exists here in the United States as in no other place on earth. THAT – we should celebrate.

Another legacy would be good health practices. We have the early maritime explorer, Captain Cook, to thank for discovering the importance of good nutrition and cleanliness aboard ship in order to prevent disease. Before Cook's time, scurvy – caused by prolonged deficiency of Vitamin C – debilitated entire crews. Cook's crews were kept healthy because he kept the living spaces on board clean and dry, provided adequate clothing and shortened 'watch' times, which reduced fatigue. He also fumigated his ships frequently and had his crews gather fresh greens, meat, fish and shellfish to supplement their diet at every call ashore. He greatly influenced other ship captains.

And, of course, the history of the U.S. Public Health Service is to be applauded. Certainly challenges lie ahead as we embark on this new century, but youngsters and some grown-ups, I might add, still need to be taught the importance of cleanliness in disease control. Washing our hands is just as important as joining our hands in friendship. And good, simple nutrition practices are important. Grandmother's admonition to practice moderation and variety in all aspects of life still stands as good advice.

Abuse of our environment hurts all life. We have long neglected a sustainable balance between the needs of nature and humanity. Humans are no more important on this planet than are salmon or Douglas fir. The Pacific Northwest has been blessed by Mother Nature, and we humans have been the recipients of her bounty. It's time for us to allow the earth to heal, practice sustainable living, and tread lightly into the future. On June 19, 2000 an article by Jim Middaugh and Tommy Brooks about saving salmon appeared in *The Oregonian*. That article included a "Fish Friendly Pledge" that gave some great rules for us today: It reads, "I pledge to:
> Plant native vegetation and use alternatives to pesticides and herbicides,
> Sweep instead of hose down streets or driveways, Compost yard debris,

Disconnect downspouts and use drip irrigation, Conserve heat and water, Use nontoxic cleaners, Drive less, Wash cars where water is recycled, Recycle motor oil and Volunteer to clean up river banks and plant trees." Sound advice. And I might add, hang your wash on the line to dry.

THE KNAPPTON COVE HERITAGE CENTER was established with all the above in mind. It's important to learn about the past – the bad as well as the good, the sad and the happy, the dumb and the smart. Accurate historical interpretation of this site is our goal – a place where you can take a step back in time and gain an appreciation of our past so that we can relate better to our future.

NOW WHAT? 2012 UPDATE

The story of Knappton Cove was first copyrighted in 2002. Great progress has been made in the ensuing decade. It became apparent that in order to further the preservation of this national historic site, we needed to alter our course of action. We needed HELP! First, we were fortunate to enlist some experts to evaluate the site and prepare a Preservation Plan. John Goodenberger and Jay Raskin filled those shoes. That plan gave us a blueprint for necessary and historically acceptable improvements.

Big, crucial and expensive projects loomed ahead. The old hospital building – our museum – needed a new roof, gutters and downspouts and a new, stable foundation. All five porches were rotting and needed replacing. In order to secure funds for these and other improvements, we decided to establish the KNAPPTON COVE HERITAGE CENTER (KCHC) as a private non-profit organization – a 501 (c) (3). That would allow us to seek grant money and accept tax-deductible donations. We secured that designation in 2005 and set up a required Board of Directors and a 25-year lease to the non-profit.

It worked! Thanks to major grants from THE KINSMAN FOUNDATION, other significant grants from the Washington Trust for Historic Preservation, the Wahkiakum Community Foundation, U.S. Bancorp, Pacific Council of Governments (PCOG), Washington Humanities and hundreds of individual donations, those major improvements have been made. This year a heating system was installed – thanks again to THE KINSMAN FOUNDATION. There is also a Scenic ByWays grant pending for improved heritage and directional signage and viewing deck with interpretive panels overlooking the river. A proposed Columbia-Pacific Passage – a 27 mile trail starting at the old town site of Knappton and ending in Long Beach—will link historic, cultural and scenic sites with coordinated signage.

A beneficial partnership has developed between the KCHC and the Historic Preservation School at Clatsop Community College. CCC students, under the guidance of their instructor Lucien Swerdloff, have made studies of the old building with recommended improvements and have reconstructed the rotted porches. We look forward to additional restoration projects in cooperation with CCC. We have also

Clatsop Community College Porch Project

gained recognition and support from Oregon State University, Portland State University and the University of Washington.

Special events are planned each year and have attracted good media coverage and increased museum visitations with between 50 to over 100 in attendance. Our two biggest events are an annual Celebration of Historic Preservation month in May and an end-of-the-season event in November "O, How Horriable is the Day" commemorating the Lewis & Clark Expedition's adventures on the North Shore of the Columbia. Both those events are enhanced by Pacific NW Living Historians who are included in our organization as part of our mission and outreach goals.

Media coverage has surpassed all expectations. Local support has been especially supportive. A segment about the Station was filmed by Public Television's *Oregon Field Guide* in 2005 and first aired that October. It has been repeated many times and continues to generate a great deal of interest and museum visitations. A number of USPHS

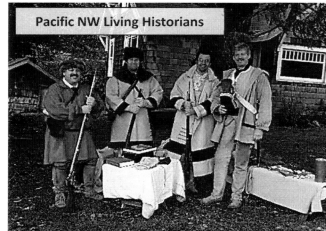
Pacific NW Living Historians

artifacts have been donated to the museum and all the displays have been upgraded and enhanced. We also have a website to further our outreach. Check out the season schedule: www.knapptoncoveheritagecenter.com or www.columbiariverquarantinestation.com.

Our Board of Directors set a goal in 2005 to have the Quarantine Hospital (aka lazaretto or pesthouse) preserved and stabilized by 2012 – to mark the 100 year anniversary of the old building. That has been accomplished. We continue to look forward to more improvements – certainly the heritage/interpretive signage, a 'Healing Garden' that is in the works, historically accurate landscaping as well as interesting programs and special exhibits to entice more visitations. With more funding, the KCHC could hire a part-time manager which would allow an increase in museum hours. Partnerships with the National Park Service and Washington State Parks remain another good option.

Come Visit!

At this point in time, we remain an all-volunteer organization – depending on grants, donations and lots of volunteer time and effort. Our Board of Directors is solid – with plenty of talent and energy. The future of historic preservation and its economic benefits are becoming more apparent. We think our future is exciting. We welcome you to our journey as we move forward into this historic preservation adventure.

Bibliography & Sources

Ambrose, Steven. *Undaunted Courage,* New York: Simon & Shuster, 1996.

Appelo, Carlton E. *Knappton, The First 50 Years.* Deep River, Washington, 1975.

Brix, Jack. PHS Officer in Charge of NW Quarantine District, retired. Correspondence & source for document *"U.S. Public Health Service, Division of Foreign Quarantine Training Section":* Rosebank, New York City. 1996

Brooks, Douglas. *"Reenacting Lt. Broughton's Survey of the Columbia River."* Astoria, Oregon: Columbia River Maritime Museum "The Quarterdeck" Vol. 19 No. 1 Autumn 1992.

Berg, Larry. Quarantine Inspector, retired. Correspondence relating to the Public Health Service.

Carmichael, D. A.; Perry N.V. & Parsons, A. L. *General Report on United States Quarantine Stations: Report on the Physical & Administrative Equipment at Astoria, Oregon.* Washington: Bureau of Public Health Service., June 25, 1915. Cofer, L.E. Assistant Surgeon General. *Public Health Bulletin No. 55 "A Word To Ship Captains About Quarantine, an Open Letter To Ship Captains."* Washington: Government Printing Office, 1912.

Columbia River Quarantine Station Log. Astoria, Oregon, 1906-1938 and related news articles from Anna Kuzmanich Washer, Public Health Clerk, Astoria, Oregon.

Cox, Ross. *Adventures on the Columbia – An Overland Journey of the Fur Trade.* Portland, Oregon: Edited & reprinted by Binford & Mort, Originally published in 1831.

Crandeall, Julie V. *The Story of Pacific Salmon.* Binford & Mort 1946.

Estoos family interviews. 1998-2000.

Harry, DeWitt. Article Published in *The Oregonian, "Quarantine Guards Port From Disease: Ships and Aliens Must Pass Muster as Fit Before Entering Columbia."* Portland, Oregon, October 2, 1921. From Anna Kuzmanich Washer, PHS Clerk, Astoria, Oregon.

Penner, Liisa. Historical Research . Archivist, Clatsop County Historical Museum, Astoria, Oregon.

Marshall, Don B. *Oregon Shipwrecks.* Portland, Oregon: Binford & Mort, 1984.

Martin, Mildred Crowl. *Chinatown's Angry Angel- The Story of Donaldina Cameron.* Palo Alto, California: Pacific Books, 1977.

Middaugh, Jim & Brooks, Tommy. *"Fish Friendly Pledge" The Oregonian.* Portland, Oregon, June 19,2000.

Mullen, M.D., Fitzhugh, *Plagues & Politics.* New York: Basic Books, Inc. 1989.

Parascondola, Ph.D., John. PHS Historian. Correspondence, photographs, historical records, Ellis Island brochures and documents including *"The U.S. Public Health Service, A Proud History"* and *"The Public Health Service"- Some Historical Notes."*

Rose, Mary Lee. *The Sou'wester: The Norwegians of Eklund Park.* South Bend, Washington: Pacific County Historical Society, Inc., Summer 1997.

Ruppell, Byron. *"A Heroic Figure of the Age of Exploration.", "Captain James Cook, a Great Navigator in the Offing" and "Scurvy."* Astoria, Oregon: Columbia River Maritime Museum " The Quarterdeck" Vol. 23 No.2 Spring 1997.

Smith, Courtland L. *Salmon Fishers of the Columbia.* Corvallis, Oregon. Oregon State University Press, 1979.

Snyder, Gerald S. *In the Footsteps of Lewis & Clark.* Washington D.C. National Geographic Special Publications, 1970.

Strong, Emory and Ruth. Edited by Herbert K. Beals. *Seeking Western Waters, The Lewis and Clart Trail from the Rockies to the Pacific.* Portland, Oregon: Oregon Historical Society Press. 1995.

Dale Treusdell with Nancy Anderson next to the PHS flag he donated to the museum.

Treusdell, Dale, Retired PHS. USPHS Documents, Books and Flag.

Weathers, Larry. *The Sou'wester: The Columbia River Quarantine Station at Knappton Cove.* South Bend, Washington: Pacific County Historical Society, Inc., Autum 1982. Additional notes from his personal file including interviews with Harold Hagerup, Clarence Bell and Anna Kuzmanich Washer. 1978-1979.

Williams, M.D. Ralpj Chester, Asst. Surgeon General. *The United States Public Health Service 1978-1950.* Washington D.C.: Commissioned Officers Assoc. of the USPHS. 1951.

Today's View of the Columbia River from Knappton Cove

Saddle Mountain

Astoria, Oregon

Dolphin (nautical term): A cluster of several pilings that form a very substantial mooring.

"Family Tree"

Far away on the open sea, lies a place for me to be
    beyond my childhood history, a place of mystery.
Stories and the pictures tell, sounds to hear and scents to smell,
    but on these pages I cannot dwell; I long to be free.

To talk and sing of foreign sands, to touch the ground and join hands
    with the people of the different lands. People like you; people like me.

As I look at my family, bouncing on my father's knee,
    my mother as she touches me, catching all my tears.
Though it hurts to think of long good-byes and a farewell drink,
    I know that I am on the brink of new frontiers.

To talk and sing of foreign sands, to touch the ground and join hands
    with the people of the different lands, People like you; people like me.

    Pray for us all, as we go afar
    Seeking our own stars under God above
    Remembering the land we love.

And time's the only one to tell, where we stood, where we fell
    our hopes, our dreams, our self-made hells make up our family tree.
A thousand miles we will roam; being together will be our home,
    the desert sand and the ocean foam, we'll see what we can see.

We'll talk and sing of foreign sands, we'll touch the ground and join hands
    with the people of the different lands. People like you; people like me.

Far away on the open sea, lies a place for me to be
    beyond my childhood history, a place of mystery.

Words and Music
by Rev. Dr. Ken Henry © 2002
(Author's son-in-law, seen here
as 'Clark' at a special event at
Knappton Cove)